PRAISE FOR
HOW TO TEACH: ENGLISH

Chris Curtis is the ideal teacher-writer, and in *How to Teach: English* he effortlessly manages the artful balance of packing in sage insights alongside a range of very practical approaches.

Funny, wise and imminently useful, this is a book from which every teacher of English – from nervous newbies to seasoned veterans – can plunder a wealth of ideas. So, no matter if you are perennially busy: put down your pile of marking and gift yourself this readable gem.

Alex Quigley, Senior Associate, Education Endowment Foundation and
author of *Closing the Vocabulary Gap*

Chris' book is an excellent manual for new and experienced teachers alike. His mixture of wisdom and experience blends together to provide teachers of English with a number of ideas that they can use in the classroom. It is a timely text, one which encourages practitioners to love what they teach – and is ideal for dipping in and out of, allowing readers to turn their attention to the chapters which cover their teaching focus at the time of reading. It is also packed full of signposts to interesting works of literature, which are perfect for the busy English teacher looking for some inspiration with the texts and topics they're using in a lesson or during a unit of learning.

Amy Forrester, English teacher and Head of Year, Cockermouth School

Curtis' smart and shrewd guide to English teaching is a welcome reminder of the potent, and too often untapped, wisdom and expertise of those at the chalkface who have learned through many years of careful and thoughtful trial and error.

For me, the greatest strength of this book lies in its central message: that English teaching is about the communication, sharing and generation of ideas, and that what matters most is the quality of thinking that happens within an English classroom. To top it off, Curtis gifts us a dazzling array of simple approaches that will guide all English teachers – from the fresh-faced newcomer to the grizzled staffroom-cynic – towards nurturing and getting the very best out of their students.

How to Teach: English really is a fabulous read. I cannot remember the last time I took so many notes when reading an education book. Needless to say, I recommend it to all teachers of English.

Andy Tharby, author of *Making Every English Lesson Count*

How to Teach: English is packed full of practical ideas for the English classroom. Chris' knowledge and experience shine through in his writing, as he shares what he demonstrably knows will work in practice and provides really sound advice for trickier areas of the curriculum.

This is a timely book – schools wanting a renewed focus on the application of the curriculum would do well to start here for their English faculties.

Sarah Barker, English teacher and Assistant Head Teacher, Orchard School Bristol, and blogger

Why, you might wonder, should I invest in yet another book on the teaching of English? This is a relatively crowded marketplace – and although there are many excellent books aimed at English teachers, none are so rooted in the subject as this one. Chris Curtis communicates not only his years of experience but also his infectious enthusiasm for a subject and an occupation he so clearly loves.

How to Teach: English is studded with an astonishing array of practical ways into the study, and the teaching, of all forms of literature as well as the nuts and bolts of language. Every page is illuminated by the gentle, guiding hand of someone who has been there, made all the mistakes you have made and survived to pass on the distilled wisdom and warmth of a true aficionado.

This is my new favourite book on English teaching – it will enhance the practice of any teacher of English, no matter what stage they are at in their career.

David Didau, author of *Making Kids Cleverer*

How to Teach: English is clever, wise and highly practical. Awash with creative prompts and pragmatic advice, it is an accessible and entertaining read which deserves its place on the creaking bookshelves of any English teacher.

Dipping in, you'll find the kinds of ideas that make you think, 'I wish I'd thought of that.' At the same time, Chris' obsession with self-improvement shines through. Full of humility, honesty and mischievous humour, this is a book about getting better by – to paraphrase the title of Chris' hugely influential blog – learning from mistakes.

It includes an ambitious and comprehensive list of chapters – focusing on key areas such as writing, grammar, Shakespeare and poetry – and illustrates the necessity of building knowledge and questioning our assumptions about our students' prior learning. With his approach, Chris places a relentless focus on the writer's craft and the power of words, advocating a sensible balance of high challenge, accessibility and creativity.

Quite simply, *How to Teach: English* is a guide to what excellent English teaching looks like – so whether you're a trainee teacher or a battle-hardened veteran, this is an indispensable resource.

Mark Roberts, English teacher, blogger and writer

This is a magnificent book that really gets to the bones of teaching English. It manages the remarkable feat of scoping the panorama of the subject: its magic, its power and its potential to take students to other worlds. And set against the big picture are commentaries on, and brilliant examples of, how to bring English lessons to life in the classroom.

How to Teach: English should be essential reading for all engaged in teaching, not just of English but of other subjects too – everyone will take something from the precision, the wit and the humanity of this terrific book.

Mary Myatt, author of *Hopeful Schools*, *High Challenge, Low Threat* and *The Curriculum: Gallimaufry to Coherence*

HOW TO TEACH

Novels, non-fiction and their artful navigation

English

CHRIS CURTIS
EDITED BY PHIL BEADLE

independent
thinking press

First published by
Independent Thinking Press
Crown Buildings, Bancyfelin, Carmarthen, Wales, SA33 5ND, UK
www.independentthinkingpress.com

and

Independent Thinking Press
PO Box 2223, Williston, VT 05495, USA
www.crownhousepublishing.com

Independent Thinking Press is an imprint of Crown House Publishing Ltd.

Page 132: extract from *The Guardian*, The Titanic is sunk, with great loss of life (16 April 1912) © Guardian News & Media Ltd, 2019. Pages 150–151 extract from W. Shakespeare, *Julius Caesar* (Ware: Wordsworth Classics, 1992, [1599]) has been reproduced with kind permission. Pages 155–156 extract from W. Shakespeare, *Romeo and Juliet* (Ware: Wordsworth Classics, 1992, [1595]) has been reproduced with kind permission.

Edited by Phil Beadle

British Library of Cataloguing-in-Publication Data
A catalogue entry for this book is available from the British Library.

Print ISBN 978-178135312-7
Mobi ISBN 978-178135330-1
ePub ISBN 978-178135331-8
ePDF ISBN 978-178135332-5

LCCN 2019932889

Printed and bound in the UK by
Gomer Press, Llandysul, Ceredigion

ACKNOWLEDGEMENTS

I'd like to thank the following people for helping me on my journey:

The English teachers I have worked with and alongside: Sam, Oisin, Chloe, Laura, Ann F., Nicki, Jas, Ian, Fiona, Sharon, Rhonda, Sally, Sue, Janice, Linda, Lorna, Sheridan, Steve, Anne B., Jenny, Delphine, Cliff, Gideon, Pat and Gill.

The English teachers who taught me: Mrs Keeling, Mr Powell, Mr Bic and Mr Ross.

The teachers on Twitter who have supported me or who have helped my thinking over the years.

Fiona Folan and David Bunker for their support and help.

I'm grateful for the generosity of my fellow professionals in sharing their experience and ideas, which has inevitably influenced my practice and, thus, the strategies I share here. I have tried to acknowledge the source of all contributions to my thinking, but if I have overlooked anything, or anyone, please trust that this is in genuine error.

A special thanks to Phil Beadle for offering me this great opportunity.

And, last of all, I'd like to thank my wife, Chloe, and my daughters, Niamh and Mya, for putting up with me.

FOREWORD BY PHIL BEADLE

English teaching can sometimes, and sadly, be the province of the unthinking trope: the thing the majority does that is both quite silly and very rubbish. Particular bugbears of mine are students being taught stock phrases that stack up like meaningless tautologies, making exam answers comprehensibly silly. Writing 'This clearly shows' about poetry (it clearly doesn't) and scribing parades of de-contextualised conjunctive adverbs as discourse markers (furthermore nothing, moreover less) being only the ones that have got my goat this week.

It is a shame that an honourable profession filled with teaching's finest accepts this waffle as being in any way deserving of anything other than lots of red pen. And such practices lead one into the direction of a search for an answer. What does anything mean? Who am I to trust here? Where is the voice of seasoned reason?

Chris Curtis entered the periphery of his editor's sight perhaps eight or nine years ago with a blog called *Learning from My Mistakes*. This title encapsulated, for me, a trustworthiness and humility that has become the alkaline to the acidity of my own arrogance. Chris does not delude himself into regarding himself as any form of pale English teaching deity. He's just a bloke (though a lovely one). But he's a bloke who's been teaching English for quite a long time, who does so to the best of his abilities and who is always on the lookout for new ways of saying things.

The sum total of that experience is included in this book. The beauty of having the thoughts of an experienced head of English for younger teachers is that Chris has thought quite deeply about some of the tropes of our profession; he has fallen down many of the same holes, made all the same mistakes, screwed up in the same manner as you, dear reader. The process of his path towards something significantly greater than competence has been taken with soft steps and, through this manner of being, Chris located a hunger in his gentility and has become that rarest of things in English teaching: an original voice worth listening to.

Chris has ideas that you can use. They are good. They are interesting. They are clever. Sometimes, they are funny. He is beholden to no one other than his students and his colleagues, in an unheralded school in an unheralded part of the country, who he 'clearly shows' that he dearly adores.

And the beauty of those ideas is that they don't take a great deal of setting up. Chris is a busy head of English; he hasn't got time for the overly wieldy. Also, you can use those ideas without having to buy into some grand ideology. I've used some of them this year in a school near the bottom of the league tables and even the recalcitrant and reckless gain enlightenment as a result. Chris Curtis has learned, and continues to learn, from making daily mistakes. Now learn from him and go and make different ones.

CONTENTS

Acknowledgements .... *i*

Foreword by Phil Beadle .... *iii*

Introduction 1

1   How to Teach Poetry 7

2   How to Teach Writing – Part 1 51

3   How to Teach Novels 75

4   How to Teach Essay Writing 109

5   How to Teach Non-Fiction 125

6   How to Teach Shakespeare 141

7   How to Teach Students to Analyse Texts Effectively 163

8   How to Teach Accuracy 179

9   How to Teach Grammar 187

10 How to Teach Writing – Part 2 203

Conclusion 235

Afterword 237

References and Further Reading 239

Recommended Websites 243

Index 245

INTRODUCTION

When my editor and I discussed this book, I told him that I wanted to write about a practical and honest approach to teaching English. I am not a guru nor Jedi master. Nor am I one of those overpaid CPD consultants, sporting a shiny suit and spouting inspirational quotes. I am a bog-standard teacher who finds suits horribly constricting, and, on any given Tuesday, probably have mayonnaise down my tie. In terms of building my educational camp, I am less bothered about the paint and soft furnishings than I am about the bricks and mortar.

I am writing this as a teacher who has thought about his practice, and about how it can be improved to help the students learn as well as they might. This book is therefore nothing more (and nothing less) than a collection of practical approaches you can use in your classroom. I have used them all in mine and, in this book, I discuss the thinking behind them and how they could be adapted. Plus, they are quick and easy and you don't need to invest a whole weekend in preparation. You'll not need to spend the school's budget to fund them, and you'll not have to wade through numerous pages of waffle to find just one idea.

I have explored many ideas and thoughts in this book. Some you might agree with. Some you might not. However, I am always happy to discuss what works, what doesn't and why. Collectively, teachers should be asking these questions, and we should explore the impact of our decisions, considering whether commonly used practices are as effective as we think. That was my intention when I started writing a blog back in 2012. It was entitled *Learning from My Mistakes*, and my thinking was, why should an NQT have to make the same mistakes that I have?

For I have made mistakes in the classroom, and I hold my hands up to that. I don't mean simple errors like getting a student's name wrong or forgetting to use the 'correct' colour pen for marking. I mean mistakes like teaching a novel without thinking about the assessment from the start. I've taught texts that were too easy and some that were *possibly* too hard. We don't acknowledge the mistakes we make in teaching often enough. There's a sense of pride in the profession: a male (or female) bravado that stops us fessing up to ourselves.

Why do NQTs make mistakes that more experienced teachers (forgetting that we too started from that point) might think are glaringly obvious? It's because we don't discuss them enough. Mistakes are seen as weaknesses, not as opportunities to learn something. If we don't explore them, how can we expect students to learn from theirs? What do we want our students to learn? How to talk about the mistakes made and find possible solutions to the problem. That's what I hope this book, and my blog, does. I am not writing this as a highly paid literacy consultant, from a gold chair perched on the lifeless bodies of former colleagues. I am writing this as a teacher who is going back into the classroom tomorrow. That is unless you are reading this during the holidays, then I will be back in at the start of term, probably with mayonnaise down my front.

So, what have I learned from my mistakes that I would pass on for others to avoid?

1. DON'T SPEND TOO MUCH TIME ON RESOURCES

When teaching *The Merchant of Venice* several years ago, I spent a good few hours making fifteen sets of three envelopes look just like the caskets that Portia's suitors have to open. The effect was spoilt in the sixty seconds it took me to hand them out. One student opened theirs and revealed to the class what was in them.

Put simply, the time spent on a resource has got to be proportional to the use you will get out of it. I have resources that I use again and again, such as a sheet listing opening sentences from various novels. I use this with Years 7, 8, 9, 10 and 11. If you want to spend time on resources – which can be fun in a strange way – make sure that you will get the due returns on them. A resource that can be used for all or most classes is better than a one-off for a poem you'll never teach again.

The lesson on *The Merchant of Venice* didn't amount to much as I had to hastily cobble together half a lesson to replace the discussion I was hoping the envelope activity would produce. It taught me that we can all too easily get caught up with making things engaging or fun when, in fact, the text itself is the puzzle. Shakespeare's riddles are the key resource, not my pitiful attempts to create props. Now, several years down the line, I'd probably put all the riddles down on a sheet of paper or on the board and add these questions:

- Which chest is gold? Silver? Lead?
- Which chest contains Portia's image and hand in marriage?

The riddles are engaging enough without half a tub of glitter and three hours' worth of prep. Engage with the students intellectually and you have got them for the lesson. Dumb down intellectual ideas and you'll have to work harder to maintain that level of thinking. *And* you'll have to create more resources. Intellectual engagement is free, paperless and easy to conjure up.

2. TECHNOLOGY IS A TOOL AND JUST THAT

I once lost a year's worth of resources due to a memory stick being put through a 40° cotton wash several times. I cannot describe the pain, anguish and suffering I experienced. I lost several units of work in the blink of a spin cycle. That's why – now – I back everything up and send it to my mum via email just in case I lose it.

Technology helps teaching, but it doesn't replace it. If your practice is too reliant on technology, then step away from it. Only the other week, I had someone use my room and change the settings on the computer so I couldn't use my PowerPoint of 'Ozymandias'. Plan B didn't work because the projector wouldn't show the YouTube video. I was left with a paperclip and a pack of lined paper and, in true MacGyver fashion, created a fairly good lesson. Without the technological fripperies we were able to focus on the text.

A computer doesn't make a lesson function. The teacher's brain does. And that only rarely breaks down.

3. PARENTS ARE NOT THE ENEMY

It's easy to forget that parents want the best for their children when you're constantly being bombarded with less than pleasant emails. Parents have fears, worries and anxieties for – and relationships with – their children. If a child is upset, they will naturally act to protect. Behind every parental complaint or issue is a reason. Understand the reason and you'll understand the parent.

One of the key difficulties in teaching is that we deal with so many humans: the young people we teach and the adults who love them most. The happiness of one is reliant and dependent on the other. And, dear reader, children are not always the most vocal of individuals. I'd advise all teachers to talk to parents. Chat with them and discuss issues. The problems I have had were usually caused by not openly discussing an issue so that it became something bigger at a later stage. Parents are people.

4. DON'T REINVENT THE WHEEL

I've spent thousands of hours making resources, and it has taken me over a decade to learn to use the people around me to help me get through the job. Teaching is hard, but all too often we don't utilise what's around us. A textbook can be part of the lesson. A colleague can help you plan and resource a lesson. It is about give and take. Give to others and it is easier to take.

The problem with teaching is the constant pace. It is just too fast and too busy. In the rush of things, it is difficult to be friendly and considerate. Occasionally, you can be too busy even to pee. Seek out resources and collaborate with others to make your work–life balance better. The job can swallow us up, and it is our collective responsibility to make sure that doesn't happen.

5. DON'T BOTTLE THINGS UP

Teaching is an emotional job. The majority of the time, we are trapped in a classroom with thirty human-shaped sticks of emotional dynamite. They could explode at any point and, as adults, we have to maintain a certain dignified restraint. We can't really burst into tears every time a student is either nice or unpleasant to us. Emotionally, we live on a knife edge. Here, it is good to talk, to discuss and to share thoughts and feelings. Do it over a drink. Do it after playing football. Just get it out of your system.

Oh, and one last bit of advice. Find a hobby and work hard to do it whenever and wherever you can. If you have no outside interests then you will become the job. That hobby might be reading, stamp collecting, painting, swimming, even naturism; but, whatever it is, keep at it and find the time for it. Don't let school make the things you enjoy become expendable. I have witnessed numerous teachers working both Saturdays and Sundays to keep on top of the job, which, after all, is just that – a job. Something that pays the bills. Regardless of how good or how bad you are, the cogs of the education machine will keep turning without you. It happens to us all. We'd like to think being a teacher is a vocation and a calling, but I haven't met that many teachers who'd be willing to teach for free.

HOW TO USE THIS BOOK

Teachers are busy people and I've written this book with that in mind. It is a rarity for teachers to be able to sit down for a long time, and it is even rarer for a teacher to be able to sit down and read. Therefore, I've kept things quite concise. The time you spend trying to visualise an extended metaphor that is spread over several pages could be better spent on friends and family. So feel free to dip into chapters that are most relevant to something you are currently teaching or read from cover to cover.

Finally, just a quick note on the poems and literary extracts used throughout. These are mainly sourced from Project Gutenberg online editions as these are so easily accessible, and the precise wording quoted here matches these sources. However, please do check whether there are any slight textual variations between these and any other edition you might be using before exploring the text with a class.

Chapter 1
HOW TO TEACH POETRY

The ability to teach poetry is held up by many as the measuring stick of a good English teacher, and this is possibly why so many lesson observations or job interviews use poetry as the subject. If you can't teach an aspect of the English curriculum with a poem, then you may not be up to the job.

A poem is a grenade of ideas and techniques in one small, perfectly formed unit, the impact of which can be far-reaching. Established teachers will have hundreds of poems in their arsenal, ready to teach as one-off lessons or as part of a scheme of work. They are often the go-to option when inspiration has packed its bags and slumped away. (Or you've had a late night!)

My advice to all new English teachers is to make a folder of poems you can use in lessons. Like push-ups in PE, the poem is a staple exercise: easily resourced and quickly done. 'Come on, give me five stanzas.'

My first attempts to teach poetry were comical. Once, as a student teacher, I attempted to cover three rather complex poems in a single lesson as the class' established teacher looked on smiling. Another time, I spent the best part of three lessons trying to teach just one poem really well. Three lessons on a six-line acrostic about animals is probably not the most demanding for a GCSE class. Understanding poetry, in itself, is a fine art: an art that's taken me years to perfect. Well, I say perfect; I really mean, be better than I originally was.

Here's the poetry manifesto I've written to share with students:

You might not be a Victorian lady mourning the loss of a child. You might not be a famous playwright with an attraction to a woman who is not your wife. You might not be a poor young man who watches his friends die in a war. But each and every one of those experiences has connections to your life. You have loved and *lost things. Poetry is about communicating experiences. Poetry teaches you how to deal with things. It might be a relative, a pet or a fluffy-ended pen you really liked to write with, but we can all recognise and identify with loss. Poetry shows you how others have dealt with a situation. Poetry is emotional and intelligent problem solving. Poetry teaches you that you have similar experiences to others in our society. Poetry explores how humans think and feel.*

The job of an English teacher is sometimes just to make students see the relevance of what they are doing. Teenagers rightly question why we do certain things. Why do we study Shakespeare? Why do we have to do poetry? Our job is about building that relevance into the lesson. We need to make that connection. That building of connections has been misinterpreted as a 'hook' or a 'starter' – or, even more dangerously, as a 'fun' activity. Fun is a word bandied about by parents, students and teachers. The danger comes when we seek simply to draw out the 'fun' aspect of learning, because learning is tough. If we wrap it up in a nice, fluffy, pretty way, we create a false impression of what real work is. Focusing on the relevance is a much better starting point.

In the classroom, teachers have to work on that relevance and connection. Yes, students have varied and different lives to us, but we need to work on building up their experiences. There has been a relatively recent focus-shift in education to the concept of cultural capital; the particular sort of cultural knowledge that one generally obtains through having experiences. Experience-rich and experience-poor students are immediately evident in any classroom: one child might make frequent visits to London; another might never have been. A recent GCSE exam question featured a woman working in London and leaving Oxford Circus. One student in my class wrote that the woman had just left a circus. A simple assumption to make. What caused it? A lack of knowledge caused by a lack of experience. Knowledge and experience are closely linked and our role, as teachers, should be to increase the former by increasing the latter.

Take a poem like 'Dulce et Decorum est' by Wilfred Owen. There are many different ways an English teacher might inform students' experience of the poem.

1   Making a personal connection – perhaps a student's relation is in the armed forces?

2   Making an intellectual connection – do you know what really happens on the battlefield?

3   Making an emotional connection – how would you feel about fighting in a war?

Before you start with anything whizzy, creative or 'fun', think about the relevance of the poem to the students. Open their eyes. How does it feel to lose a child, for instance? Ben Jonson's 'On My First Son' explores this awful reality and, like much of the canon, we can use it to teach young people empathy with another's tragedy.

Often, the first step is to ask what the ideas or questions in a poem are. In English, as I often say to my students, we develop our thinking and we explore how others think. Where better to see that than in poetry? A poem is pure, undiluted thinking or feeling. A poem is an idea. A poem is a thought. A poem is a feeling bottled.

Why is it that humans turn to poetry in the happiest, or the saddest, of times? Let's get married – what poem shall we read? Tom has passed away – what poem shall we read? Our inability to express a thought or feeling is helped by poetry. I can't possibly express how sad I am, but this poem does, so you can see how I am thinking and feeling at this exact moment. This writer expressed what I can't possibly articulate. The emotional dimension of a poem is one we can easily ignore, but is hard to forget when you have been affected and moved. How many times do we ask students what a poem makes them feel? Not often enough, I'd venture. The fear is that students will default to the predictable 'it's boring' response. In a way, it sounds slightly unnatural. 'Eh, Jamal, Mr Curtis has gone a bit funny. He's talking about feelings.'

Being a teenager is difficult. Over the years I have taught a fair few angry ones (regardless of gender) and what always strikes me as telling is how each and every one of them is usually struggling to articulate what they are thinking or feeling. As a result, they either fight the system or fly from the classroom. We know that many of our students are struggling with identity, pride, peers, sexuality, feelings, thoughts and life choices at this point. For this reason alone it is so important that we explore the articulation of emotions. I recall my own teenage years, and some adult ones, where I felt something, but couldn't define it. The wider world doesn't help either. Society seems to be telling young people that there are two valid categories of emotion: love and hate. We love things and so post them on Facebook with glee, or we hate things enough to raise a pitchfork and join a mob in protest. We have become binary. Things are either positive or negative, good or bad, joyous or depressing. There are no stages in between. Poetry can be a daily source of emotional literacy to help students understand that there are thousands of different emotions we might experience at different points in our lives. When teenagers are struggling, the English teacher provides an opportunity to articulate and name those feelings. It comes as no surprise that we are often fondly remembered.

We can teach students about the emotions at the heart of poetry by asking them questions:

- What does the poem make you feel?
- Which bits of the poem do you like?
- Which bits of the poem do you not like?
- Where do your emotions change in the poem?
- Why do your emotions change in the poem?
- Have you felt this emotion before?
- What does the poet want you to feel at the start of the poem?
- What does the poet want you to feel by the end of the poem?

Our relationship with literature has been affected by our society's inability to express emotional nuance. We often allow students to dumb down emotional responses as well. How many times have we heard phases like, 'it makes the reader want to read on' or, 'it stands out'? Students will easily spot techniques and maybe even the ideas at the heart of the text, yet they will rarely mention the emotional impact. They'd rather see the components than the whole and how it relates to them. So, teachers need to look at how students form relationships with texts. Those connections should be paramount, and they should be emotional. Students need to understand that a poem is an emotional journey.

Take one of the poems used in the recent AQA GCSE English literature exam: Carol Ann Duffy's 'War Photographer'. It is primarily about emotions and is slightly ironic in the way it explores how people in England aren't emotionally connected to terrible things happening to people in different countries. I spent a whole lesson with a group of less able boys talking about the emotions involved in being a war photographer before we even looked at the poem. We explored photojournalism[1] and several key images taken in different war zones. One featured a place called 'Sniper Alley' in Bosnia and another was a photograph taken by João Silva who, when on assignment in Afghanistan, stepped on a mine and was severely injured – the whole incident was captured on film. Then we explored some writing by George Orwell describing his perspective of war. As a class, we built up an emotional picture of being a war photographer. Asking the students what this must be like as a quick starter is not enough. They need to see, hear, think and feel it. Between us, we saw the idea of guilt emerge from the pictures and extracts. One boy brought up the idea of moral disgust at how you could film or photograph someone dying, unable to save them. Another boy kept asking me how one becomes a war photographer. By the time we did actually read the poem, the group were articulate in the possible emotions experienced by a war photographer, which, in turn, gave them a profound understanding of how they might want to hide from the experience while being haunted by what they can recall and angry that nobody else feels the same way. I had simply scaffolded the emotions needed to understand the poem.

In some cases, students need a bit more than just the poem to get the emotional connection; in others, they don't. The emotional dimension of a poem is one that we are quick to neglect but one that students can easily identify, extend and develop. Like the old chicken and egg scenario, which came first, the literary device or the impact? For students, it seems to be the literary device but, in reality, it is the impact. Start with the feelings and the emotions and it becomes easier to explain how the writer created them. So, what does it make us feel? How is it written to make us feel this emotion? Where it may be hard to decide if chicken or egg came first, it is easier to say that emotion comes first with poetry. The emotions are often what connects us to the poems.

Poetry as a form of text is arguably the strongest and most powerful. I'd go even further to say it is often one of the most easily accessible forms of writing. But its enigmatic quality can cause problems for students. Somehow, there's nuanced

---

1   *The Guardian*, The shot that nearly killed me: war photographers – a special report (18 June 2011). Available at: https://www.theguardian.com/media/2011/jun/18/war-photographers-special-report.

meaning underneath the similes and metaphors; a secret initially hidden from the students' view.

As a child, I felt I was broken. During the 1990s, it was common to have magic eye posters in your bedroom. These were a form of optical illusion with a picture hidden within a pattern. For the life of me, I could never find the hidden picture. This is how students can feel when presented with a poem: that they must find the single hidden meaning when there are actually several. The teacher's job is to sift through those meanings, present all of them and let the student come to their own conclusion.

As a golden rule, I like to start with what the student thinks a poem is about:

- What do you think it is saying?

- What, in your opinion, is it teaching us?

- How do you see this differently to your partner?

Teach students that poetry is about multiple meanings and multiple feelings. All too easily a poem becomes a bag of techniques which are loosely linked together. Poems are about thoughts, feelings, ideas, knowledge and experience – and our job is to allow the students to own all of these.

1. WHAT IS THE POEM'S CENTRAL QUESTION?

Take William Blake's 'The Tiger' (a poem I hold close to my heart as it was the first one I ever taught to a class).[2] On a simple level it is about a tiger, but it contains so many different meanings.

---

2   This is one example of the point made at the end of the introduction: here the source text uses the spelling 'Tiger', but it is also common to see this spelt 'Tyger'.

The Tiger

Tiger, tiger, burning bright
In the forests of the night,
What immortal hand or eye
Could frame thy fearful symmetry?

In what distant deeps or skies
Burnt the fire of thine eyes?
On what wings dare he aspire?
What the hand dare seize the fire?

And what shoulder and what art
Could twist the sinews of thy heart?
And, when thy heart began to beat,
What dread hand and what dread feet?

What the hammer? what the chain?
In what furnace was thy brain?
What the anvil? what dread grasp
Dare its deadly terrors clasp?

When the stars threw down their spears,
And watered heaven with their tears,
Did He smile His work to see?
Did He who made the lamb make thee?

Tiger, tiger, burning bright
In the forests of the night,
What immortal hand or eye
Dare frame thy fearful symmetry?[3]

---

3   W. Blake, 'The Tiger', in *Songs of Innocence and Songs of Experience* (Project Gutenberg ebook
    edition, 2008 [London: R. Brimley Johnson, 1901]), pp. 51–52. Available at: http://www.gutenberg.org/
    files/1934/1934-h/1934-h.htm#page51.

To simplify things, we could suggest that the poem is about three questions:

1   How impressive is the tiger?

2   How could somebody create a creature like the tiger?

3   Is the tiger stronger than God?

Informing the poem is the Romantic poets' view of the sublime: the fear and awe evoked by nature and its power. Blake looks at the tiger with a thrill and excitement that is tinged with fear. This links to the frustration some Victorians felt with the Industrial Revolution, which seemed to present a dark and scary future, filled with smog and factories. Some mourned the loss of the natural world.

The ideas at the centre of the poem are universal: ideas, in fact, that all students can connect with.

· Have you ever seen an animal and been impressed by it?

· Have you ever seen something and felt that it was too perfect somehow?

· Have you seen something that has scared and excited you at the same time?

The teacher's job is to light the fire of curiosity and to make those connections concrete. You have a wealth of thoughts and feelings you can tap into. Take some of the poems in the new AQA GCSE poetry anthology, for instance:

'London' by William Blake – How do you react to the poor when you see them in the street?

'Ozymandias' by Percy Bysshe Shelley – What do you think the prime minster will be remembered for in 100 years' time?

'The Charge of the Light Brigade' by Lord Alfred Tennyson – Is it a noble thing to sacrifice your life for the good of the country?

Never forget that poetry is about thinking. Start with thinking, and then build on the thinking to do some more thinking. Once you show students that poems can incorporate many different ideas and feelings, they are not limited to looking for a correct one. Teach students to see that there is no right or wrong, just better and even better readings of a poem. If Frank thinks that 'The Tiger' is about little green men, get him to convince the rest of the class by providing evidence from the text.

Additionally, it is helpful to remember that coordinating conjunctions are your friends when talking about poetry, or indeed any text. As in life, there are normally several things going on at once. The poem is about X *and* Y. The poem explores A *or* B. That complexity needs reaffirming with the students.

Finally, students often fear committing to definitive answers. That is why questions are a really useful entry point; they aren't concrete. Get students to think of the questions being asked in the poem. Even the shyest of students can give you a question.

2. INFERENCE WORDS

To deal with complex ideas, students need vocabulary to properly articulate complex thinking. The big difference between a very able student and an able one is in the subtlety of the former's use of vocabulary. If we take 'The Tiger' again, what happens if we introduce the words 'inferior' and 'superior'? Who in the poem is which or what?

Inferior: voice/reader/tiger/God?

Superior: tiger/God?

The interesting thing is that, as soon as you introduce a choice of vocabulary – generally, abstract nouns work best – you start to develop and extend their thinking and the complexity of their ideas. Just by introducing the words 'inferior' and 'superior', you can completely change a student's understanding of the poem.

The poet makes the tiger seem superior to the reader and, by the end, makes even God seem inferior when he uses the word 'dare'.

These words change the interpretation of the poem. It is now about power and a battle between two entities. Look again and you'll see the poem is full of this imagery.

Getting students to use abstract vocabulary to summarise a text is a powerful tool. I often call these 'inference words': ones that don't necessarily appear in the text, but allow us to infer something about it. What is really going on? Take this poem:

The Eagle

He clasps the crag with hooked hands;
Close to the sun in lonely lands,
Ring'd with the azure world, he stands.
The wrinkled sea beneath him crawls;

He watches from his mountain walls,
And like a thunderbolt he falls.[4]

Of course, you could make the same inferences about power. 'The Eagle' is quite similar to 'The Tiger'. In addition to 'superior' and 'inferior', you could add inference words such as 'sadness', 'power', 'control', 'regal' and 'godlike'. Suddenly you have a greater level of engagement with the text. The vocabulary students use to describe ideas is important and it is up to us, as teachers, to develop this ability. Depending on the level of the student, you can develop the level of understanding through vocabulary:

- powerful
- superior
- omnipotent

Each word has a different shade of meaning, and they build in complexity. That's why vocabulary is so important. The same question with one different word changes the level and type of understanding.

---

4   Lord A. Tennyson, 'The Eagle', in J. C. Collins (ed.), *The Early Poems of Alfred Lord Tennyson* (Project Gutenberg ebook edition, 2012 [1851]). Available at: http://www.gutenberg.org/files/8601/8601-h/8601-h.htm#section96.

- How does the writer show us that the eagle is powerful?

- How does the writer show us that the eagle is superior?

- How does the writer show us that the eagle is omnipotent?

Think of the words you'd use to describe the poem, because you can raise the quality of understanding simply through your own use of vocabulary. After all, you could always take a word and go one step further. What if I used the word 'biblical' to describe 'The Eagle' and 'atheist' to describe 'The Tiger'? Now, Blake was religious, and 'atheist' isn't a word you might generally associate with him, but this gives you a starting point for discussion. To what extent is the poem religious? We can then introduce to students the fact that Blake was against organised religion and the constricting nature of its formal structures. How does that change our understanding of the poem? Maybe words like 'biblical' and 'atheist' don't help us to describe the poem precisely, but they do help us to then search for the right word to describe the idea. Blake isn't denying the existence of God, but questioning how something so large and powerful can be controlled, contained and 'framed'. We can then add words like 'spiritual' and 'agnostic' to the mix.

One simple word has the power to transform the meaning of a text and to develop, improve or alter a student's understanding of a poem.

3. CH ... CH ... CH ... CHOICES

When you have established what the writer is saying, the next logical step is to look at how they are saying it. If there is one thing students can do with aplomb, it is spot techniques.

Teacher: What is interesting about how the poem is written?

Student: Well, it has alliteration, repetition and a simile.

Teacher: What is really interesting about how the poem is written?

Student: I've already told you – it has alliteration, repetition and a simile.

I call this 'technique vomiting' and it tends to be the default setting for a lot of students. It isn't necessarily a bad thing, but it can be if other aspects of their powers of analysis are underdeveloped. If a student can't explain a choice, then their technique spotting is worthless. Joining meaning with technique is paramount.

Offer students a choice, and then get them to explore the underlying reasoning. For example:

Why did Charles Dickens call Oliver Twist Oliver and not Olivia?

A simple choice can get students to begin to think like a writer. So, why didn't Dickens make Oliver Olivia? Of course, it is down to Dickens being famously cruel to his characters. He couldn't be as cruel to an Olivia as he could be to an Oliver. Or would the text have taken on a more darkly sinister undertone if a young female had been at the mercy of the cruel male adults?

Let's take another poem by William Blake, into which I have thrown a few variations in wording.

London

I/we wander/walk/stroll through each chartered/narrow street,
    Near where the chartered Thames does flow,
A mark in every face I/we meet,
    Marks/scars of weakness, marks/scars of woe/misery.

In every cry of every man,
    In every infant's cry of fear/sadness,
In every voice, in every ban,

The mind-forged manacles I hear:

How the chimney-sweeper's cry
   Every **blackening**/gleaming church appals,
And the hapless soldier's sigh
   Runs in blood down palace-walls.

But most, through midnight streets I **hear**/see
   How the youthful harlot's curse
Blasts the new-born infant's tear,
   And blights with plagues the marriage-hearse.[5]

Often with texts I explicitly draw to a class the specific choices made by the writing. We know that there are lots of options available to a writer, but I like to place two choices together: the first, the writer's original choice (the choice underlined in the poem); the second, an alternative option posed by me. Students then discuss why the writer chose one option over the other. Look at the verb 'wander', for example. Why would the voice wander rather than gallop, walk, run or move in any other way? To wander is to walk quite slowly and take things at one's own pace. This verb alone suggests that the voice is not rushing and is purposefully taking their time as to experience things and notice every sight and sound. It could also suggest a lack of urgency, which could hint at the relaxed nature of the voice's approach to life.

As a generic approach, alternative comparisons work with all types of text. More able students tend to see the nuanced intention behind the choice. Offering students an alternative gives them a point of comparison. Take the difference between 'sob' and 'cry'. They mean much the same thing, but there's a slight difference; sobbing tends to be more physical and louder than crying, and a bit snottier too!

Boy A cried over the football match.

Boy B sobbed over the football match.

---

5   W. Blake, 'London', in *Songs of Innocence and Songs of Experience* (Project Gutenberg ebook edition, 2008 [London: R. Brimley Johnson, 1901]), p. 58. Available at http://www.gutenberg.org/files/1934/1934-h/1934-h.htm#page58.

The use of 'sobbed' suggests that Boy B was more upset than Boy A. They were both upset, yet B tangibly more so. A nuanced change but one that is incredibly important in the new English language GCSE. Understand the precise meaning of a word and you understand what is going on beneath the surface. More able students tend to have a greater appreciation of the options a writer has. They see the alternatives and can identify why a writer would use sob instead of cry. That's why students should read as much as they can to develop their vocabulary and enable them to see these alternatives.

Experience refines our ability and potential. Providing alternative choices helps kick-start understanding by acknowledging experience gaps. Plus, it avoids the need for technical terminology to express complex thinking. A student can articulate the reason behind their choice in their own words.

Of course, giving students a choice also empowers them, putting them in a position where they have to make concrete decisions while touching upon abstract concepts.

Some further examples of choice could include:

- Suggest alternative titles for the poem – 'The City'/'Divide'/'The Industrial Revolution'/'A City of Contrasts'.
- Write your own version of the whole poem/a stanza/a line.

I do enjoy writing my own version of a poem. Students then have to decide which the genuine one is. Here's my attempt with 'Futility' by Wilfred Owen.

> ### Futility
> *France 1915*
> *He might not be dead;*
> *there's a chance that his soul's not fled.*
> *Maybe the Sun's rays will wake*
> *His spirit.*
>
> *Snow's claws clasp him tight*
> *but the Sun's fingers*

caress
his cold body.

Basking in the Sun, there's hope.
Maybe on this cold morning its power will awaken him.
The Sun knows.
The Sun's power makes plants grow.
If it makes life, then surely it can coax this body back to us.

Are his limbs too cold to be warmed?
Why ever did the Sun warm this cold Earth and give it the breath of life?

And the vastly inferior original:

Futility

Move him into the sun —
Gently its touch awoke him once,
At home, whispering of fields unsown.
Always it woke him, even in France,
Until this morning and this snow.
If anything might rouse him now
The kind old sun will know.
Think how it wakes the seeds —
Woke, once, the clays of a cold star.
Are limbs so dear-achieved, are sides
Full-nerved, — still warm, — too hard to stir?
Was it for this the clay grew tall?
—O what made fatuous sunbeams toil
To break earth's sleep at all?[6]

---

6   W. Owen, 'Futility', in *Poems* (Project Gutenberg ebook edition, 2008 [1918]). Available at: http://www.gutenberg.org/files/1034/1034-h/1034-h.htm#link2H_4_0022.

I don't consider myself a poet, but doing this gives students the opportunity to consider what makes poetry poetry. Usually they spot the dud. But, every so often they don't. In any case, they always have to justify their opinion.

The Sun's power makes plants grow.

Think how it wakes the seeds—

This allows for comparisons on a linguistic and figurative level. My simplistic and reductive explanation doesn't capture the humanised nurturing power of the sun. It is easier to explain the effect when you have a point of comparison. If you are very lucky, you may be able to find draft versions of certain poems. A starting point for draft copies of poems are biographies of the poets and the internet. The British Library has kindly digitised many draft manuscripts, which can be found by searching their website.[7]

I often take this further and offer choices to students explicitly. What do they think warrants exploration in a given text? Recently, with one group, we spent time looking at the way Roald Dahl, J. K. Rowling, Charles Dickens and Robert Louis Stevenson use characterisation in their writing. My students came to the opinion that Dickens was obsessed with appearance whereas Rowling was more bothered about personality and Dahl more concerned with character. Stevenson, however, based on *Treasure Island*, was interested in the physical flaws in a character and their actions. Choices are everywhere in the classroom, and in texts, and if we don't offer them to students we are in danger of producing boring lessons.

Perspective

Some choices, such as perspective, are staring students in the face. Perspective is, to put it simply, the position we see things from. Whose voice is speaking to us? Whose glasses are we looking through? From what angle are we observing things?

---

7 See https://www.bl.uk/.

The choice between a male or female narrator has a massive implication for the meaning of a poem. So too can the narrator's age; does the poet choose experience or innocence? I find it helpful to extend this questioning by looking at the *impact* or *effect* of perspective. Why does the writer use the first person perspective?

- First person – personal/relationship building/connecting/understanding/sharing/close.

- Second person – instructing/direct/showing.

- Third person – observing/distancing.

I have found that an emphasis on specific words relating to effect works better than a list of sentences or phrases. Students love a catchphrase and that's why we get endless 'it makes the reader read on' or 'it stands out' answers. Precision with words supports precision with ideas. Let's take 'connecting' as an example. We know what the word means, but it isn't one we employ when talking about poems. Yet it is a word that explains the effect of text. A student can then say that 'London' is about connecting – connecting us to how the voice experiences London, connecting us to the inequality of the city and how it has been imposed by the state, and connecting us to the plight of the inhabitants. When students have this word at their disposal they can explore all the ways in which the poem connects with the reader. How is it connecting to the reader?

Offering choice allows students to see the way the text is built up, brick by brick. Students need just a few 'choice bricks' to help them build a meaningful interpretation. The principle of chucking everything at them and seeing what sticks isn't always the best one. I prefer to give students three or four precise words to explain an effect, impact or choice as a starting point. Time will allow them to do this automatically themselves, but in the meantime they need our guidance, support and instruction.

Verse and free verse

The form of poetry can be tricky to explain. Explain why the writer used a dramatic monologue. Umm ... they wanted to make it dramatic, and they wanted to make it a monologue. It is sometimes hard to explore the use of form. That's probably why we spend a lot of time telling students why the writer used a sonnet, a dramatic monologue or a haiku to express their love. I find it is often more meaningful to look at the distinctions between verse and free verse.

- Verse – organised/regular/planned/structured/trapped/concrete/systematic/ thoughtful.

- Free verse – disorganised/irregular/spontaneous/unrestricted/abstract/ unsystematic/thoughtless.

Relate this to the poem 'London' and we see that the tight use of verse and the form of four-line stanzas could reflect the sense of entrapment. There is a rigid structure at the heart of London: people are manacled to one way of thinking, and misery is systematic; there is a higher power causing it.

On the alternative side, we have free verse and Walt Whitman's 'After the Sea-Ship'.

After the Sea-Ship

After the sea-ship, after the whistling winds,
After the white-gray sails taut to their spars and ropes,
Below, a myriad myriad waves hastening, lifting up their necks,
Tending in ceaseless flow toward the track of the ship,
Waves of the ocean bubbling and gurgling, blithely prying,
Waves, undulating waves, liquid, uneven, emulous waves,
Toward that whirling current, laughing and buoyant, with curves,
Where the great vessel sailing and tacking displaced the surface,
Larger and smaller waves in the spread of the ocean yearnfully flowing,
The wake of the sea-ship after she passes, flashing and frolicsome
    under the sun,
A motley procession with many a fleck of foam and many fragments,
Following the stately and rapid ship, in the wake following.[8]

---

8   W. Whitman, 'After the Sea-Ship', in *Leaves of Grass* (Project Gutenberg ebook edition, 2008 [1855]). Available at: http://www.gutenberg.org/files/1322/1322-h/1322-h.htm#link2H_4_0113.

'After the Sea-Ship' lacks the rigid structure and form of 'London'; the sea is unpredictable and the men on the ship are at its mercy. The poem presents the sea as playful and we might conclude that the use of free verse reflects that playfulness with its varying lines and false ending. 'Under the sun' seems a natural end point, yet Whitman carries on.

Both poets present man as subject to some higher power: the playful sea and the manacles of the mind. The use of verse reflects the ideology. Man is in awe of nature in Whitman. He is at the mercy of societal control in Blake.

Rhyme

Students can have a complex relationship with rhyme. The younger ones tend to gravitate towards poetry that rhymes, yet analysis of the rhyme rarely features in their exploration.

- Rhyming – unnatural/planned/lyrical.

- Un-rhyming – natural/spontaneous.

The use of rhyme in 'London' is slightly jarring for me. Rhyme is usually upbeat and melodic but here it details unpleasantness and is marginally unsettling, heightening the sadness of the themes. It is only in the last line of the first verse that we are introduced to the misery of the place and its 'woe'. Blake builds up to this with the harmless 'street', 'flow' and 'meet' and then reveals the poem's true intent in something of a bathetical manner. The next verse uses rhyme to stress negative words like 'ban' and 'fear'. The third stanza takes this negativity further: 'cry', 'appals' and 'sigh'. Only one of the rhyming words isn't negative. In the last stanza, we get 'curse', 'tear' and, finally, 'hearse'. The last word is a negative one.

Letting students see the choices the poet made is meaningful because it gives them the tools to analyse texts independently. Teaching students to analyse a simile allows them to talk about similes, but it doesn't get them to explain the reasons behind the choice. Explaining why the poet used a metaphor instead of a simile reveals a more complex understanding and leads you to more detailed reasoning. In 'London' simile wouldn't be sufficiently committed, insufficiently totalitarian. Metaphor gives a more determined and dogmatic viewpoint so there's no doubting Blake's opinion. Metaphor provides clarity.

4. STRIPPED BACK POEMS AND LAYERING

How you introduce a poem can be important. An emphasis on engagement can neglect the fact that there is such a thing as intellectual engagement. Such an emphasis has meant I've seen poems introduced with chocolates and with shocking videos featuring even more shocking acting from the teacher. But not everything needs a stimulus.

Engagement is a funny thing. I could sit in a meeting looking like I am being bored to tears, but actually I am deep in contemplation. On the outside, I might look like I'd rather be anywhere else. On the inside, I'm thinking of solutions to the age-old problem of whether Year 11 should go on study leave or not. You'd be hard pushed to tell whether I am engaged unless you speak to me. Young children are transparent with their levels of engagement but, as they turn into teenagers, this becomes visibly less apparent. You can't always tell if a student is engaged fully or not. Teenagers often keep their thoughts to themselves and hide any signs of enjoyment.

It is always interesting to learn what students enjoy (or not) over the course of the year. You only know this when you talk to them. Imagine every student is showing you their 'poker face'; they won't show you their 'tell', so you'll need to dig deeper. True intellectual engagement is not visible, though questions and comments might indicate it. For this reason, I think we need to be cautious about 'false engagement'. The five hours you spent creating an albatross from toilet roll for your mimed version of 'The Rime of the Ancient Mariner' could be replaced with five seconds at the photocopier and presenting the text to the students. Engage their brains first and the excitement, fun and joy will be the result of their thinking.

Approach 1 – the highlights

When introducing a poem for the first time, what you present to the students is important. Give them the complete text of Tennyson's 'In Memoriam' or Coleridge's 'The Rime of the Ancient Mariner' and you can imagine the fear and trepidation they feel. As with wine, you sometimes have to decant a poem and let it breathe. Some, however, are more like vodka shots and best ingested quickly.

Take this poem by Rudyard Kipling. It explores the treatment of old soldiers by various parts of society. Here I have presented some highlights from the poem: a few select lines placed in the order that they appear.

Tommy

[1] *I went into a public-'ouse to get a pint o' beer,*

The publican 'e up an' sez ,"We serve no red-coats here."

[2] *I went into a theatre as sober as could be,*

They gave a drunk civilian room, but 'adn't none for me;

[3] *You talk o' better food for us, an' schools, an' fires, an' all:*

We'll wait for extry rations if you treat us rational.

[4] *An' it's Tommy this, an' Tommy that, an' anything you please;*

An' Tommy ain't a bloomin' fool—you bet that Tommy sees![9]

Having two daughters myself and years of teaching other people's children under my belt, I am aware of how popular culture is engineered to grab young people's attention. In the modern age, we have to work harder to get students to notice things. That means blocking out some channels. Over the years, I have watched students analyse texts and they are often drawn to the most obvious parts: the beginning and the end. But there's meaning in every word, line and verse, so reading parts in isolation helps students to see this clearly.

---

9   R. Kipling, 'Tommy', in *The Works of Rudyard Kipling: One Volume Edition* (Project Gutenberg ebook edition, 2000 [1914]). Available at: http://www.gutenberg.org/files/2334/2334-h/2334-h. htm#link2H_4_0058.

If we look at the first line of 'Tommy', we see the context of the poem. A solider is refused a drink in a pub. We see that the poem is told from his perspective. We also infer that he lacks education because he has an informal way of speaking. When we look at the second section, we see how he is shunned by people in a theatre. The fact that a 'drunk civilian' is allowed entry highlights the ridiculous nature of the way he is treated. The last section contrasts the promises he was given with Tommy's view of the reality of the situation.

Looking at a poem in a compartmentalised way helps to build those concrete ideas. It gives students a firm base from which they can explore the poem in greater depth. You can, and there is no problem with it, give students the full poem and get them to analyse it. But this approach helps to structure the reading in a way that secures a clear understanding of the key ideas without students being swamped by swathes of text that needs decoding. It's similar to the *Reader's Digest*[10] approach to books: a condensed and reduced version of the text that allows for ease and speed, without removing the key ideas. For us, this approach allows students to get to the heart of the poem and then allows them to develop that understanding when faced with the full text.

The full poem is here:

Tommy

I went into a public-'ouse to get a pint o' beer,
The publican 'e up an' sez, "We serve no red-coats here."
The girls be'ind the bar they laughed an' giggled fit to die,
I outs into the street again an' to myself sez I:
  O it's Tommy this, an' Tommy that, an' "Tommy, go away";
  But it's "Thank you, Mister Atkins", when the band begins to play,
  The band begins to play, my boys, the band begins to play,
  O it's "Thank you, Mister Atkins", when the band begins to play.

I went into a theatre as sober as could be,
They gave a drunk civilian room, but 'adn't none for me;

---

10 An American publisher who produced condensed versions of books.

28

They sent me to the gallery or round the music-'alls,
But when it comes to fightin', Lord! they'll shove me in the stalls!
*   For it's Tommy this, an' Tommy that, an' "Tommy, wait outside";*
*   But it's "Special train for Atkins" when the trooper's on the tide,*
*   The troopship's on the tide, my boys, the troopship's on the tide,*
*   O it's "Special train for Atkins" when the trooper's on the tide.*

Yes, makin' mock o' uniforms that guard you while you sleep
Is cheaper than them uniforms, an' they're starvation cheap;
An' hustlin' drunken soldiers when they're goin' large a bit
Is five times better business than paradin' in full kit.

*   Then it's Tommy this, an' Tommy that, an' "Tommy, 'ow's yer soul?"*
*   But it's "Thin red line of 'eroes" when the drums begin to roll,*
*   The drums begin to roll, my boys, the drums begin to roll,*
*   O it's "Thin red line of 'eroes" when the drums begin to roll.*

We aren't no thin red 'eroes, nor we aren't no blackguards too,
But single men in barricks, most remarkable like you;
An' if sometimes our conduck isn't all your fancy paints,
Why, single men in barricks don't grow into plaster saints;
*   While it's Tommy this, an' Tommy that, an' "Tommy, fall be'ind",*
*   But it's "Please to walk in front, sir", when there's trouble in the wind,*
*   There's trouble in the wind, my boys, there's trouble in the wind,*
*   O it's "Please to walk in front, sir", when there's trouble in the wind.*

You talk o' better food for us, an' schools, an' fires, an' all:
We'll wait for extry rations if you treat us rational.
Don't mess about the cook-room slops, but prove it to our face
The Widow's Uniform is not the soldier-man's disgrace.

*   For it's Tommy this, an' Tommy that, an' "Chuck him out, the brute!"*
*   But it's "Saviour of 'is country" when the guns begin to shoot;*

29

> *An' it's Tommy this, an' Tommy that, an' anything you please;*
> *An' Tommy ain't a bloomin' fool—you bet that Tommy sees!*[11]

Of course, I would then look at the poem in more detail. Having made the starting point clear, I then get students to see what is added in the rest of the text. How does it link? Does the text support, build on, challenge or contradict what has been revealed already?

Approach 2 – methodical reading

By the time students get to secondary school, a lot of assumptions are made about their reading skills. We automatically assume that they will be able to read. This approach – methodical reading – is one I use to help students, and it combats something that a lot of teachers are guilty of doing: neglecting gaps in understanding. All too often, we tell students to focus on the 'gist' of a text and not to worry about the bits they don't understand. We gloss over the problem areas and hope that through osmosis, symbiosis or something else ending in 'osis'[12] the student gets the poem. This approach combats that and it reflects the way I tend to approach all texts, and I've done this little experiment with hundreds of English teachers. Take the poem below and annotate it, as you normally would (unless this is a library book).

The Kraken

> *Below the thunders of the upper deep;*
> *Far, far beneath in the abysmal sea,*
> *His antient*[13], *dreamless, uninvaded sleep*
> *The Kraken sleepeth: faintest sunlights flee*
> *About his shadowy sides: above him swell*
> *Huge sponges of millennial growth and height;*

---

11 R. Kipling, 'Tommy'.
12 Editor's note – thrombosis?
13 Original spelling from the source.

And far away into the sickly light,
From many a wondrous grot and secret cell
Unnumber'd and enormous polypi
Winnow with giant arms the slumbering green.
There hath he lain for ages and will lie
Battening upon huge seaworms in his sleep,
Until the latter fire shall heat the deep;
Then once by man and angels to be seen,
In roaring he shall rise and on the surface die.[14]

I have seen many different types of analysis, including some pretty bizarre ones. The way we annotate a text reveals something about how we read. There are a few common approaches:

- line by line

- spotting techniques

- questioning

They are all acceptable processes for what is essentially decoding a text. And, they are all fine for mature, sophisticated readers like yourself. The line-by-line method suggests that the reader is meticulous and mechanical and possibly doesn't see the whole text but instead a puzzle to unlock. They might stop reading when they are faced with a bit they don't get. The spotting techniques method reveals a focus on the immediate features, which can fail to engage with the content, ideas and meaning of a text. This reader will be great at noting points about a text but will fail to develop these. The questioning method shows engagement with the ideas. I often walk around during a mock exam to see how students engage with a text, and I look at the papers afterwards. Their annotations tell us so much. How close they are. And how far away.

---

14 Lord A. Tennyson, 'The Kraken', in J. C. Collins (ed.), *The Early Poems of Alfred Lord Tennyson* (Project Gutenberg ebook edition, 2012 [1851]). Available at: http://www.gutenberg.org/files/8601/8601-h/8601-h.htm#section125.

We have to explicitly model how to read, yet there isn't a uniform process for reading a poem. Children go from one teacher to another, adopting their way, or cobble something together themselves. You can see how this has the potential to cause confusion. In my current school we follow a standardised methodology for reading a text.

1   Spot things we don't understand (words, lines, phrases).

2   Summarise what the text is about. Then answer the following questions.

3   What is the purpose of the text? For poetry, we'd rephrase it to: what is the message of the poem?

4   What is the reader supposed to think and feel?

5   What is interesting about the language choices made by the writer?

6   What connections are there between parts of the text? What else does this connect to outside the lesson?

For me, this method has been transformational. Because students are starting from a point of inexperience, it is easier for them to begin with what they don't understand than what they do. The number of hands that go up when I ask a class what they don't understand about a poem far outweighs the number when I pose the antithetical question. You create a shared exploration with the first question: we are working this thing out together. At this point you can also assess understanding and clarify meaning. Occasionally, something challenges your assumptions. I had one student struggle with the word 'trial', something that I would have assumed they'd know. They weren't familiar with it. We can't start the reading by assuming we know where the gaps in knowledge are. The other beauty of this approach is that it takes little preparation. You just need a copy of the poem on a sheet of paper or a PowerPoint slide.

Approach 3 – mystery

'There's been a ... murdah! I mean murder.' That's how I introduce Robert Browning's poem 'Porphyria's Lover'. I reveal the poem one section at a time, asking students to tell me what happened, who has been murdered and why.

> [1] *The rain set early in to-night,*
>
> *The sullen wind was soon awake,*
>
> *It tore the elm-tops down for spite,*
>
> *And did its worst to vex the lake:*
>
> *I listened with heart fit to break.*

During the whole set-up, we return to the question of the murder. Who is victim? What is the motive? I add extra questions as we go along and I also get students to ask questions themselves. There's nothing like a murder mystery to get the grey cells working.

- Why is the environment perfect for a murder?
- Who do you think the narrator is?

Students often pick up on the aggression and the negativity of the environment. Then we explore concepts such as foreshadowing and pathetic fallacy. We might even explore how the pathetic fallacy links with the narrator's 'heart'. One ghoulish student usually makes the point that in this weather nobody can hear you scream, so a murderer could easily get away with their crime.

> [2] *When glided in Porphyria; straight*
>
> *She shut the cold out and the storm,*
>
> *And kneeled and made the cheerless grate*
>
> *Blaze up, and all the cottage warm;*
>
> *Which done, she rose, and from her form*
>
> *Withdrew the dripping cloak and shawl,*

And laid her soiled gloves by, untied
Her hat and let the damp hair fall,

- Who is the murderer?
- Who is the victim?
- How does the poet build up the tension here?
- What aren't we seeing at the moment?

[3] *And, last, she sat down by my side*
And called me. When no voice replied,
She put my arm about her waist,
And made her smooth white shoulder bare
And all her yellow hair displaced,
And, stooping, made my cheek lie there,
And spread, o'er all, her yellow hair,
Murmuring how she loved me—she
Too weak, for all her heart's endeavor,
To set its struggling passion free
From pride, and vainer ties dissever,
And give herself to me forever.

- Why does the narrator remain silent?
- What is the relationship between the two people? Is it an equal relationship?

[4] *But passion sometimes would prevail,*
Nor could to-night's gay feast restrain
A sudden thought of one so pale
For love of her, and all in vain:

So, she was come through wind and rain.

Be sure I looked up at her eyes

Happy and proud; at last I knew

Porphyria worshipped me; surprise

Made my heart swell, and still it grew

While I debated what to do.

- Why does the narrator's heart swell?
- What is the narrator 'debating'? Why is he undecided?

[5] *That moment she was mine, mine, fair,*

Perfectly pure and good: I found

A thing to do, and all her hair

In one long yellow string I wound

Three times her little throat around,

And strangled her. No pain felt she;

I am quite sure she felt no pain.

- Why strangle her? Why not kill her by another method?
- Why is it important she felt 'no pain'?

At this point, you usually get a mixture of surprise and disbelief as students try to work out if it is possible for someone to be strangled with their own hair. And you get one or two students looking at the girl with the longest hair with a longing expression.

[6] *As a shut bud that holds a bee,*

I warily oped her lids: again

Laughed the blue eyes without a stain.

And I untightened next the tress

About her neck; her cheek once more

Blushed bright beneath my burning kiss:

I propped her head up as before,

Only, this time my shoulder bore

Her head, which droops upon it still:

The smiling rosy little head,

So glad it has its utmost will,

That all it scorned at once is fled,

And I, its love, am gained instead!

- Why is it so important that her eyes were 'without a stain'?
- Why does he kiss her now and not before?

[7] *Porphyria's love: she guessed not how*

Her darling one wish would be heard.

And thus we sit together now,

And all night long we have not stirred,

And yet God has not said a word![15]

- What is the narrator's motive for killing her?
- Why do you think 'God has not said a word!'?

The poem is dark, but proves how a mystery really gets students engaged. After working through the poem, we then look back to see which clues indicate that there was something wrong and how the situation developed. This approach leads to some very precise analysis to ascertain meaning. There's no need to draw attention to specific words as the text itself, and the mystery element, draws students to look closer. They

---

15 R. Browning, 'Porphyria's Lover', in H. E. Scudder (ed.), *The Complete Poetic and Dramatic Works of Robert Browning* (Project Gutenberg ebook edition, 2016 [Cambridge, MA: The Riverside Press, 1895]), p. 286. Available at: http://www.gutenberg.org/files/50954/50954-h/50954-h.htm.

might make inferences about the fact that she never says hello when she enters, or they might look at more subtle word choices. The dramatic monologue allows for a shift in focus: in the first half, the students are trying to work out what is going to happen, and in the second half, work out why it happened.

Approach 4 – Scanning a poem

To explain the process to students, I use a hospital analogy: a range of technical scans can be used by doctors to identify a problem (CT, MRI, X-ray) and each scan records a specific structure within the body. If you want to look at bones, you would X-ray the body. If you want to look at the brain, you would use an MRI scan. I apply that level of scan to poetry. We scan a poem with a particular focus. All you need is a copy of the poem on an A3 sheet of paper and some pens. As with approach 2, students methodically analyse the text, usually working in pairs or groups, annotating it using a series of questions. For the student with a pencil case full of coloured pens this is a joy because for each layer they can use a different colour. The idea is, again, to then bring the different components of the students' understanding together. I give them five minutes for each layer. At the start, I give students the question we are going to answer. Something like: how does the writer convey loneliness in the poem?

Layer 1: looking at how the poem is written

- What do you notice about how it is written?

- What is the most effective word?

- What patterns do you notice in the words?

- What is repeated?

- How is it presented on the page?

Layer 2: reacting to the poem

- What feelings do you have when you read the poem?
- Where in the poem do your feelings change?
- Do your feelings differ at the start and end?
- What questions does the poem raise?

Layer 3: surface meaning

- What is the poem about?
- Who is speaking?
- What different ideas does the voice have of the subject?

Layer 4: deeper meaning

- What is the poem teaching us?
- What is the writer trying to get us to see/understand/realise?

When the students have completed all the different layers they make connections between them. The important thing, for me, is the connection between the meaning and the language, as this is the hard part to get students to see. In this approach, they join meaning to feelings to linguistic and structural choices.

5. SONNETS AND VOLTAS

A common thing English teachers do is introduce a type of poem and then get their students to write their own. That's great, and the approach does work. However, there is value in teaching one particular type of poem really well for a number of different reasons. Step forward the sonnet.

I've taught haikus, limericks and many other forms of poetry during my time. They are sweet little things, but cognitively they do very little to push the learning on, and I've yet to see a haiku or a limerick on a GCSE exam paper. A sonnet, however, is such a powerful poem and one that will be examined. Why is it so powerful? Put simply, because it replicates what we do in English again and again: explain a thought in detail.

The sonnet is an argumentative essay, a piece of descriptive writing and an advice column all at once. It models the typical structure for explanation in writing. You have an idea, introduce a conflicting thought and then sum it up. The structure is important but once you get the basics like octave, sestet and volta, you get to look at the interesting aspects. The volta is the turning point in the poem and there are numerous types:

- Ironic – makes a point and then knocks it down.

- Emblem – describes the object/meaning of the object.

- Concessional – admits the problems or issues.

- Retrospective-prospective – moves from the past to the future.

- Elegy – grief to consolation/refusal/even more grief.

- Dialectical argument – argument, opposing argument, combination of the two.

- Descriptive-meditatative – description, memory or thought, revised description.

- Mid-course – a sharp, radical and surprising turn.[16]

---

16 A chapter is devoted to each of these in M. Theune (ed.), *Structure and Surprise: Engaging Poetic Turns* (New York: Teachers and Writers Collaborative, 2007).

There are turning points in every text we study in English, so it is meaningful and effective if we take time in lessons to explore these within sonnets. The turning point of any text can be emotional, intellectual, spiritual, logical or illogical, and is incredibly important to developing the overall meaning. However, I feel that students need to see this modelled with sonnets before they explore the turning points in other forms of poetry, and then in drama and prose texts. Where is the change? What type of change is it? Why has the writer made the change? What is the 'turning point' of *An Inspector Calls*? Define the turning point and you have a better understanding of the writer's desired impact on the audience or reader.

6. SYLLABLES 3, 2, 1

I underestimated the value of looking at the rhythm of poetry for many years. The language, for me, took priority. Look at this simile. Isn't it interesting? Look at this word. Isn't it powerful? I neglected the full complexity of the poem: it isn't just a collection of words. It is a collection of finely tuned words positioned in a meaningful way to be appealing, moving or jarring when read. All too often we focus on the linguistic rather than the aural elements as these are incredibly complex.

I tend to draw attention to the use of syllables first. At a later stage, I will introduce stressed and unstressed but, initially, I focus solely on the number. I ask students to spot where the poet uses words of three syllables. To simplify, I talk about the threes, twos and ones. Take 'Song' by Christina Rossetti:

Song
When I am dead, my dearest,
*   Sing no sad songs for me;*
Plant thou no roses at my head,
*   Nor shady cypress tree:*
Be the green grass above me
*   With showers and dewdrops wet;*

And if thou wilt, remember,
 And if thou wilt, forget.

I shall not see the shadows,
 I shall not feel the rain;
I shall not hear the nightingale
 Sing on, as if in pain:
And dreaming through the twilight
 That doth not rise nor set,
Haply I may remember,
 And haply may forget.[17]

The majority of words are one syllable with the occasional two-syllable word along the way. There are only three words in the whole poem with three syllables: 'remember', 'nightingale' and 'remember' (again). In simplistic terms, you have to put more effort into reading those words, and so place more emphasis on them. All these words end a line, which adds to the rhythmic effect. They also break the rhyme, which is inconsistent. The writer is drawing our attention to these words. So the question I ask students is: why?

The voice wants to be remembered. The rhythm makes that clear. Although the verses end with 'forget', we are drawn to 'remember' in the previous line. Why is attention drawn to the 'nightingale'? A nightingale is a common literary symbol of the connection between love and death. A nightingale can also be a symbol of happiness or sadness. It is drawing our focus towards this symbolism. When students begin to look at poems from a syllabic point of view, they can really investigate the use of patterns.

Take the following lines from 'Song':

When I am dead, my dearest,
 Sing no sad songs for me;

---

17 C. Rossetti, 'Song', in *Goblin Market, The Prince's Progress, and Other Poems* (Project Gutenberg ebook edition, 2008 [London: Macmillan and Co., 1862]). Available at: http://www.gutenberg.org/cache/epub/16950/pg16950-images.html.

I love the use of syllables here, and it is relatively simple to get students to see what is happening rhythmically. Sometimes, I work with a class to present the rhythm differently. For example:

---

1 1 1 1, 1 2,

  1 1 1 1 1;

Why does the poet end with a two-syllable word on line 1? Could it be to show the importance of the 'dearest'? She could easily have used the noun 'love' but chose 'dearest' instead. I also like the use of single syllables to create pace, almost reflecting the desire not to dwell on death. The use of one-syllable words draws attention to the simplicity or positivity of the situation. I could spend ages looking at syllables and often do. Usually, this involves me banging on tables while chanting the lines.

Then we get on to stressed and unstressed syllables. Deciding whether a word is stressed or unstressed is a nuanced thing and it is all down to the sound it makes in relation to others. A slightly louder or longer sound compared to the words around it. Often, we refer to a heartbeat to depict stressed and unstressed syllables; dee (unstressed) dum (stressed), dee (unstressed) dum (stressed), dee (unstressed) dum (stressed). I like to have an example on the board to compare other lines with. The following is from Act 1, Scene 3 of *Macbeth*:

Time and the hour runs through the roughest day.

Time / **and** / the / **hour** / runs / **through** / the / **rough** / est / **day**.[18]

When a worked example is visible, students can both see (bold equals stressed words) and hear the stressing of the words. It also means that they have a point of comparison. Does your line match the example on the board? Of course, the example here is in iambic pentameter, the most common form of meter we teach at GCSE. Although stresses can change, the example gives them a starting point. Students can see that the likelihood of the word 'the' being an unstressed word is high. I might go even

---

18 W. Shakespeare, *Macbeth* (Project Gutenberg ebook edition, 1998 [1606]). Available at: http://www. gutenberg.org/cache/epub/1533/pg1533-images.html.

further and give them a list of commonly stressed and unstressed words to aid their understanding.

A colleague of mine, Fiona Folan, adds an extra dimension by using names to make it a bit more personal.

Sha-ron

Ke-vin

Chris-to-pher

Fi-**o**-na

She uses this to introduce students to the trochee[19] and then gets them to see what happens when the stress is changed to a different syllable, introducing the iambus.[20] It works because students are so used to their names and the familiarity heightens their understanding.

Sha-**ron**

Chris-**to**-pher

I have also found it useful to present the words on the page differently. So, our line from 'Song' goes from this:

*When I am **dead** my **dear**est*

---

19 A trochee is the pattern of a stressed syllable followed by an unstressed syllable.
20 An iambus is the pattern of an unstressed syllable followed by a stressed syllable.

To this:

	I	dead	dear
When	am	my	est

It's the separation of words/syllables that is important. Why are some stressed and others not? We could say that the stresses help to assert the bluntness of the poem. There's no euphemistic approach to death here; the word 'dead' is used bluntly and is also stressed. This heightens the realistic attitude towards death that the voice has. If this was a text message, the word would be in capitals, with an emoji thrown in for good measure.

Focusing on syllables helps students to see the patterns at the heart of poetry. Meaning originates from so many different sources and techniques. Forget this and you neglect the masterplan behind the language.

7. KNOWLEDGE OF POEMS AND STYLES

Knowledge is power and knowledge of poetry is key. For years, we have neglected the explicit teaching of knowledge, seeing English purely as a skills-based subject. The rise of the use of knowledge organisers has made teachers reassess this. A knowledge organiser, for the uninitiated, is a sheet of A4 paper on which the key information about the text or topic is stored so that a student can revise and test themselves. In English, they usually contain a summary of the text, a list of characters with biographies, key quotes, key factual information and the key terms or concepts needed to understand the text. Simply, they are a study guide boiled down to one sheet of paper which students can revisit again and again. They retain the knowledge needed to access the text so students can attune to more meaningful levels of understanding. After all, how many times have we had to remind students which character did what in a text? Many students simply retell the plot in essays because they feel the need to show that they know the text. The knowledge organiser helps to address that problem and provides a bedrock of understanding so we can build knowledge on top of knowledge.

The important part is that students can recall the 'tip of the iceberg'. Remember one thing and that leads to more meaningful content. What follows is an example of the questioning format I regularly use with poems – in this case, 'Ozymandias' – to test students' recall. The first three questions relate to content. The next three to quotations and the final questions link effect with particular literary devices.

1   What remains intact from the original statue of Ozymandias?

2   What does the pedestal say people should do when they look at the statue?

3   Where is the traveller from?

4   What 's' and 'v' are used to describe the statue's face?

5   What 'a' describes the land where the statue is found?

6   What 'n' remains of his legacy?

7   What typical form of love poetry is used here?

8   What exaggerated and pompous language does the writer use to show Ozymandias' arrogance and self-importance?

9   What piece of alliteration is used to suggest how empty and neglected the statue is now?

I use the same format repeatedly in lessons. As a starter. As a plenary. As a recap. The questions are regularly revisited months after the poem has been studied. The transformation in learning is incredible. Boys love to get all the answers right and less able students feel empowered because it is a low-stakes test that is easy to answer. The great thing is that this format builds up the vocabulary associated with analysis. Plus, it provides phrases and syntactical structures for them to use in their own writing. It is so easy to do and reduces the amount of planning and preparation needed for a lesson. I have tons of these sets of questions; I even have them for each scene in Shakespeare's plays. The key is to revisit the knowledge again and again.

Year 7 knowledge organiser: exploring heroes and villains in literary texts

Synonyms for hero	Synonyms for villain	Words to explore meaning
Challenger, conqueror, defender, guardian, patron, protector, supporter, sympathiser, upholder, vanquisher, victor, vindicator, warrior, winner, idol, pioneer, daredevil, explorer	Anti-hero, criminal, devil, scoundrel, sinner, brute, creep, evildoer, lowlife, malefactor, mischief-maker, miscreant, offender, rapscallion, rascal	Suggests, implies, hints, infers, connotes, denotes, symbolises
Different types of hero	**Different types of villain**	**Colours and their meanings**
The Perfect Hero – a hero who represents the best of humanity.

The Misfit – an unlikely hero because they are unpopular or unlike others.

The Everyman Hero – a hero like everybody else – normal and makes mistakes.

The Anti-Hero – a hero who doesn't behave like a hero and does good but only for their own gain. | The Anti-Villain – a villain who has some characteristics that the reader might like.

The Authority Figure – a villain who is evil because they have power.

The Bully – a villain who takes pleasure in making the hero look bad.

The Beast – an inhuman villain: animal, creature, alien, machine.

The Corrupted – a villain who was once good. | Red – blood, danger, passion

Black – evil, hatred, soulless, determined

Grey – lifeless, boring, lacking spirit, cold

White – innocent, good |
| | **Techniques** | **Aspects of the character to describe** |
| | Exaggeration – describe things in more detail.

Ambiguity – notice different possible interpretations.

Metaphor – compare something to something else by using the word 'is'.

Simile – compare to something else by using the words 'like' or 'as'.

Pathetic fallacy – use the weather to reflect a | Clothes

Behaviour, actions

Voice, speech

Face, facial expressions

Body

Reaction to others

People's opinions of them

Entrance, exit

Belongings |

			Effect words
			Apprehensive, intimidation, superior, inferior, cautious, unease, curiosity
		character's feelings. Repetition – repeat a detail about the character.	Sentence structures/ phrases to learn
			A sense of
			A feeling of
			By using the word '____', the writer makes us …
			The use of [techniques] suggests
	The Criminal – a villain who does bad things for money or power.		
	The Disturbed – a villain with psychological problems.		
	Femme Fatale – an attractive female villain who causes men disaster.		
	Henchman – a villain who works for a mastermind.		
	Mastermind – a villain who tends to get others to do their work; they are incredibly powerful and controlling.		
The Prodigy – a hero born to be a hero, but must grow up first.	Qualities of a villain		
The Tragic Hero – a hero destined for tragedy.	Powerful, intelligent, immoral, wounded, determined, merciless		
The Trickster – a hero who defeats evil by outwitting it.			
The Warrior – a hero who defeats evil through strength.			
Qualities of a hero			
Wisdom, responsibility, fortitude, conviction, intrepidity, loyalty, courage, honesty, dedication, perseverance, compassion, focus, determination, sacrifice			

Source: provided by Chloe Pearce

47

List of poems

Here's a list of poems I've collected over the years. Some have also been recommended by friends on Twitter. I worry that, because of exam focus, students only study a narrow pool of poetry. Key Stage 3 shouldn't just be about the content of the old GCSE anthologies. There is so much more out there. Sadly, the nature of the job often prevents us from searching. All the poems listed here can catch fire in a classroom.

'As Kingfishers Catch Fire' – Gerard Manley Hopkins

'Blessing' – Imtiaz Dharker

'Carrion Comfort' – Gerard Manley Hopkins

'Child on Top of a Greenhouse' – Theodore Roethke

'Funeral Blues' – W. H. Auden

'Home-Thoughts, from Abroad' – Robert Browning

'If' – Rudyard Kipling

'Jaguar' – Ted Hughes

'Kubla Khan' – Samuel Taylor Coleridge

'Lady Lazarus' – Sylvia Plath

'Meeting Point' – Louis MacNeice

'Metaphors' – Sylvia Plath

'Mushrooms' – Sylvia Plath

'Not Waving but Drowning' – Stevie Smith

'Pigtail' – Tadeusz Rozewicz

'Scaffolding' – Seamus Heaney

'Stanley' – Lorraine Mariner

'Still I Rise' – Maya Angelou

'Still Life' – Thom Gunn

'Tell Me, Tell Me, Smiling Child' – Emily Brontë

'Text' – Carol Ann Duffy

'The Dead' – Sylvia Plath

'The Flea' – John Donne

'The Jogger's Song' – Roger McGough

'The Kaleidoscope' – Douglas Dunn

'The Man with Night Sweats' – Thom Gunn

'The Orange' – Wendy Cope

'The Schoolboy' – William Blake

'The Sun Rising' – John Donne

'To the Evening Star' – William Blake

'Torture' – Alice Walker

'Warming Her Pearls' – Carol Ann Duffy

'What It Feels Like' – Alice Walker

'Who's for the Game?' – Jessie Pope

Also check out the Poetry Foundation website for more.[21]

---

21 https://www.poetryfoundation.org/poets.

Chapter 2
HOW TO TEACH WRITING
– PART 1

Unlike speaking, writing is not a natural process. Whereas students pick up spoken language through experience and exposure, writing is a lot more complex and is primarily explicitly taught. It is difficult, time-consuming and, occasionally, quite boring. I was the kid who would rather chat and argue about a book than write about it. Like your average teenage boy, I'd spend ages procrastinating about writing. In fact, I tend to leave writing deadlines to the last minute. That hasn't changed much to this day.

The problem comes, perhaps, when we try to dress up the process, covering it in tinsel. We say it is fun and easy when, in reality, it is drawn out and blooming difficult. Personally, it took me writing every week on my blog to begin to understand how it really works. It also took me finding some good editors to make me see how to improve. One told me I needed more of an opinion, another highlighted my tendency to repeat things. I am still learning.

I think primary schools do a good job of making writing fun, but the veneer has worn off by secondary school. You are writing to make yourself understood and to present an image of yourself to another person. Some might say that writing is a dying skill, but if you look at the comments on a Facebook page or Twitter, you can see there has never been a greater need to help students, and adults, communicate articulately with the world and think about the message they are presenting to others.

There should be a balance in lessons between highlighting the areas for improvement (spelling, accuracy, grammar, content, structure) and praising what works. Students need to see success and be praised when they achieve it. Through chance, skill or mistake great writing can flow from even the clumsiest pen, but to increase the chances of that happening teachers need to ensure that there are lots of opportunities to write in lessons. We also have to overcome the thought that all writing should be

51

marked, assessed and inputted into a spreadsheet for a school leader to scrutinise. Work should be read, but it doesn't need a stamp of approval or detailed analysis from the teacher every time. An obsession with the final product can neglect the complex process of writing, which includes thinking, planning, sequencing, researching, reflecting, redrafting and fine tuning. Students need to explore and develop their voice, and that only comes with time and work on the processes involved. I have seen some students panic and worry when writing, because they are more focused on the end than the means. The fear of how the end product will be marked, and viewed, by the teacher has a detrimental impact. Rather than enjoy the process of communicating and exploring ideas, they are entrapped by their 'mind forg'd manacles'.

Our fetishism for marking has warped writing in the classroom. Teachers, if we are honest, will admit that we control the amount of work produced in a lesson so that there is less to mark. The sad thing is that this can cause us an inescapable cycle of underdeveloped work. The more we talk a language, the more fluent and confident we become in it. Equally, the more we write, the more fluent we become. We must address this and challenge how marking is used in the classroom. It shouldn't get in the way of progress and development. At the moment it *can*. Intervening during the process, for me, gets better improvements than summative marking. Why? Well, simply, in the middle of the process students are susceptible to change and willing to embrace it. As soon as we hit the end, it takes a highly responsible student to want to redraft and improve work. A discussion during the process can address the flaws of marking. Talking about what a student has done or could do will get better results than asking them to write five sentences after they have completed the work. The time before and during writing are instrumental periods of the process and when teachers should be diving in to help students. Afterwards is about learning from the process and making sure students can recall key parts, but during is when you can model, guide and support them to make changes.

What style of writing should dominate the classroom? Do we really want every student to use a clumsy facsimile of Dickens' style? Or do we want students to write in the style of Enid Blyton, or even Agatha Christie? Style is often dictated by fashion and so becomes problematic as fashions change. One teacher might particularly enjoy dystopian fiction, so their preferred style would be one of bleak description, buckets of misery and the odd shot of optimism. Another might be a fantasist and promote writing that features trolls, unicorns and mighty swordsmen. English teachers need to be cautious of their own tastes and address the matter of style head-on. Compare Dickens to Rowling. Compare Dahl to Conrad. All are successful writers, but they haven't followed a formula that says, 'Do this and you will become successful.' A sparse, subtle writer can be as telling as a detailed, bombastic, repetitive one. This forms a minor paradoxical difficulty for students.

The problem comes as a result of our exam system and how teachers have interpreted marking. Is the exam assessing a student's proficiency in a skill? Or is it assessing the student's ability to include a language feature? Skills have been neglected in favour of more easily evidenced content. Students are told that if they include X, Y and Z they will get a top grade. Evidencing content features has warped teaching and marking. If a student includes a feature, then it is evidence, I suppose, that a student *can* use it. But have they used it skilfully, appropriately, effectively or structurally? Did the student simply plonk a semicolon in because a teacher told them to throw one in like a grenade and hope it does the job? Bloated writing is rewarded by teachers and is not considered successful in academic terms unless it has numerous (clearly visible) markers. No matter what the student is writing, they have to pack it with discernible features associated with the top grade. In fact, exam boards are increasingly requesting that teachers, and students, move away from this approach and stop using content mnemonics such as AFOREST[1] and the like to instead focus on the communication of ideas.[2]

Simplicity in writing is not encouraged in schools. There are writers whose work is seemingly effortless and beautiful, with very few unwieldy words or obvious techniques, and they are the ones we should be including in lessons. For me, these include Patricia Highsmith, Angela Carter, John Steinbeck, Ray Bradbury, Iain Banks, Stephen King, Saki, George Orwell and Ernest Hemingway.

---

1   A simple acronym used for persuasive writing to ensure that students use alliteration, facts, opinions, rhetorical questions, emotive language, statistics and tone.
2   AQA, *GCSE English Language Paper 2 Writer's Viewpoints and Perspectives: Report on the Examination*, 8700, June 2017. Available at: https://filestore.aqa.org.uk/sample-papers-and-mark-schemes/2017/june/AQA-87002-WRE-JUN17.PDF.

An idea can be expressed in a single sentence or a whole paragraph.

Example 1:

Marley was dead, to begin with.[3]

Example 2:

It was the best of times,

it was the worst of times,

it was the age of wisdom,

it was the age of foolishness,

it was the epoch of belief,

it was the epoch of incredulity,

it was the season of Light,

it was the season of Darkness,

it was the spring of hope,

it was the winter of despair,

we had everything before us, we had nothing before us, we were all going direct to Heaven, we were all going direct the other way—in short, the period was so far like the present period, that some of its noisiest authorities insisted on its being received, for good or for evil, in the superlative degree of comparison only.[4]

The examples prove that there is more than one way to set the tone and scene. Where one is blunt and direct, the other is grandiose and poignant. They have similar functions but achieve them in different ways. A simple sentence can be just as powerful as a long multi-clause sentence or detailed paragraph. The key is knowing when it is best to use which option and in which context. Both are styles we should explore to help students write well.

---

3   C. Dickens, *A Christmas Carol* (Project Gutenberg ebook edition, 2006 [New York: The Platt & Peck Co., 1905]), p. 11. Available at: http://www.gutenberg.org/files/19337/19337-h/19337-h.htm.

4   C. Dickens, *A Tale of Two Cities* (Project Gutenberg ebook edition, 2004 [1859]). Available at: http://www.gutenberg.org/files/98/98-h/98-h.htm.

1. SEXY SPROUTS

Over the years, I've spent countless hours teaching the features of different text types and ended up frustrated when information only stuck in the heads of the most able students. Students with an advanced level of understanding were able to recreate texts while others were only able to copy their most basic features. I have read countless newspaper reports which have been a narrative set out in columns with a headline and lovingly and time-consumingly drawn picture. Looks like the real thing; doesn't read or sound like it.

Writing can appear close to wizardry. You are mixing a number of ingredients to make a powerful spell. It was when I was working on some persuasive writing with Year 8 that I developed what has been, for me, a monumental piece of understanding. We were watching the infamous Marks and Spencer adverts where glossy footage of food is narrated by the soft, slowly spoken, sultry voice of a woman. It made food sound sexy. We attempted to give sprouts that treatment.

Soft, silky leaves peel back to show a crunchy, hard centre. Ready for picking.

The great thing was that it made students use all of the techniques I had previously spent months teaching them ... naturally and automatically. Putting the emphasis on effect instead of text type made the writing instantly better. Instead of asking students to write 'dot-to-dot' pieces, I was asking them to make real texts with the emphasis on the impact. In truth, I was getting students to act as real writers. Real writers don't follow a set list of ingredients. They try their damnedest to communicate a thought or a feeling. I gave classes the following piece of text and asked them to rewrite it for a different effect, ranging from guilt to boredom to awe.

Pure evil. The worst vegetable in the world. A soggy, watery parcel of smelly green goo. It is as if the worst of every meal has been scooped together and boiled down into one small ball. Eating them is like eating sick that has been left out overnight and has little bits of peas floating around in it.

The discussion moved away from identifying simplistic devices. Now students were thinking, and that is the key word, about how to achieve the desired impact. They were asking the right questions instead of questioning what they needed to include. They weren't looking at writing as a shopping list.

Thanks to several students and classes for producing the following examples:

Making the reader feel impressed and awed.

Brussel sprouts handpicked by Scottish farmers. All washed in fresh, crystal clear bottled water. All the way from the waterfalls in the Scottish Isles. Feel the sensation as you bite slowly into the crispy, crunchy leaves of this round succulent wonder of the earth. These sprouts will light up any occasion. Be sure to indulge yourself on these green parcels of delight and joy.

Making the reader feel guilty.

How would you feel if you were walked past in the supermarket every day, with no one even thinking about buying you? Well, this is how Barbara and her family feel. They grew up dreaming of the open air, but when they finally got there, they were ripped and torn from their homes and were shoved in a tight, uncomfortable plastic box and stacked on shelves where nobody looks. Forgotten and unloved, Barbara waits.

Making the reader feel shocked and horrified.

At six months old, they are ripped from the safety of their family and thrown into boiling water. Their skin melts and their leaves burn away from their body. Slowly, they suffer in pain as they die in the skin-blistering water. It takes two minutes for a sprout to die in boiling water. If they are lucky, they are chopped or mashed beforehand. The majority are not so lucky and they face this agonising death.

Making the reader feel a sense of urgency and need.

Now these sprouts are limited edition. One of a kind. They come in several shades of green. Select the best one for your meal. A light green for a light, healthy meal and a dark shade of green for a decadent, rich meal. They are so versatile. From cooking to eating, there's so much you can do with these limited edition sprouts, which have been genetically engineered to be even tastier than the average sprout. But stocks are limited, so if you want to experience something new, experience something different, experience something original, then pick up a bag now. Only £5 for a bag, buy this special treat for a loved one, a friend, or even to treat yourself.

This had a knock-on impact on their creative writing. It highlights one of the problems students have: often they are limited by the 'effect' of their creative writing. How many times have I read something intended to scare me? Students tend to have two default modes: to scare or to use humour. Open them up to other effects and feelings and you'll get more interesting and, more importantly, meaningful writing. To aid their realisation, I tend to place huge emphasis on the emotional journey: write me a story that covers these three emotions – fear, disgust, pride.

2. SENTENCES

You tend to find that specific students have a penchant for particular techniques. Thomas always focuses on alliteration. Sam can spot a simile a mile off. Or, if you are lucky, as I once was, they can spot any religious reference in a text. For me, it is sentence types. I will come back to them later, as I am somewhat obsessed with them. I love finding new sentence types. I love teaching sentences. I love exploring the meaning behind the construction of a sentence.

Several years ago, I came across an idea by Alan Peat that I have used again and again. Modelling is important and the more we can do it the better for our students. I am the role model at the front of the class. I should be setting the example. Yes, you can, and should, openly make mistakes to show you are human but, importantly, you should be an example to model, mimic and copy. Just don't copy my dress sense or mannerisms.[5]

Alan's idea is simple. You take a particular grammatical structure and name it – for example: the more, the more sentence.

---

5   Or you'll end up with mayonnaise on your tie.

The more I waited, the more I worried.

You explicitly teach students the sentence construction. Help them to see how and why the sentence is constructed in that way. You can also draw attention to the use of punctuation, aiding and developing their control of the same. Afterwards, get students to create their own in isolation.

The more I looked, the more I panicked.

The more she ate, the more the people in the restaurant noticed her.

Then I get students to write a paragraph which includes the structure. Over a couple of lessons, I can cover about ten of these structures. We then write a longer text incorporating them all. All the time, I am modelling the process of writing. As I have been doing this for years, I have collated examples into a booklet for most units. They make a nice homework, starter or even intervention strategy. The students have to create three different examples using the structure in the model.

My sentence obsession is so bad that I am constantly looking for new ones. Each book I read serves up a collection to mimic and use. Teach one sentence a week and a student could have thirty different ones before the end of the year. I even get students to find and name their own. This allows them to identify the key components of sentences in a way that they can replicate in their own writing. Students are focused on the structure more than the content when they do this. For example, a student of mine named one structure a 'happy/sad' sentence.

The children laughed and giggled as the soldiers lifted the corpse off the ground.

Alan Peat has a number of different resources and apps linked to the idea and they do help students to develop and improve their writing. I'd highly recommend his *Writing Exciting Sentences: Age Seven Plus* and his website for resources.[6]

3. PARAGRAPHS

I will admit that for years I was pretty clueless about teaching paragraphs. I followed the usual party line of TIP TOP. Start a new paragraph for each change of time, place, topic or person. I would repeat this again and again, but I didn't really get under the surface until I used Alan Peat's sentence structure approach. Then I looked at how I could adapt this for other aspects of English teaching. So, I tried to name and categorise different paragraph structures and, in doing so, felt a little like a Victorian explorer pinning butterflies to a board.

On a sheet of paper, I drew several boxes and filled them and then some more. I made sheets for non-fiction and fiction. I now use them for all forms of writing with all levels of student. It provides a great starting point for writing and offers students many possible choices. After all, we don't want students to default to the typical.

Here's one such example, following the 'No ... No ... No ... No ... But, there was ...' paragraph structure:

No life had visited the room. No light had touched its fingers on the delicate wallpaper and fine paintings. No breeze had tickled the faded curtains and frail netting across the boarded up windows. No soul had experienced rest here. But, there was one movement.

---

6 A. Peat, *Writing Exciting Sentences: Age Seven Plus* (Biddulph: Creative Educational Press, 2008). His website is https://alanpeat.com/.

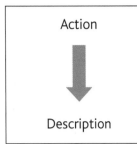

Action

Description

No ...
No ...
No ...
No ...
But, there was ...

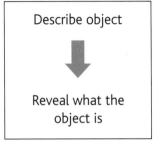

Describe object

Reveal what the object is

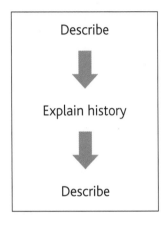

Describe

Explain history

Describe

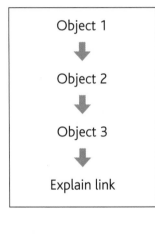

Object 1

Object 2

Object 3

Explain link

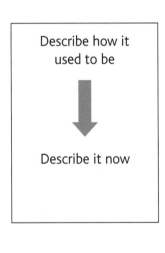

Describe how it used to be

Describe it now

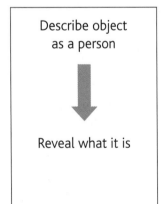

Describe object as a person

Reveal what it is

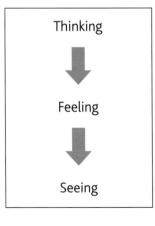

Thinking

Feeling

Seeing

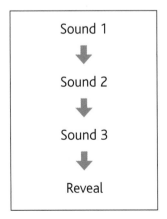

Sound 1

Sound 2

Sound 3

Reveal

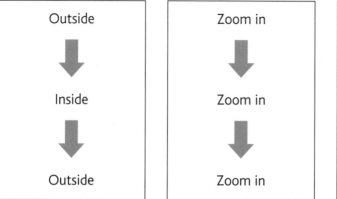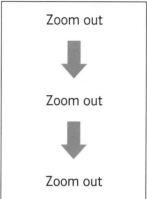

When you have a starting point, you can be more playful with the structure. I always love it when a student invents their own.

A year ago. A month ago. A day ago. Today.

A year ago, the beach was hidden from the world. A month ago, a boat arrived and people found this oasis of beauty. A day ago, more people arrived. Today, I discovered what had happened to my sanctuary.

Close, closer, closest.

Close to me was a light. It was flickering gently in the breeze. Closer still were the sounds of people, laughing and chatting. Closest to me was the person I loved most in the world.

Near, far, near, far.

I could hear my friend's breathing behind me. The enemy was on the outskirts of the city, getting closer to us by the minute. My friend's eyes showed fear and terror. The footsteps of the soldiers echoed as they entered the city looking for us.

---

4. UNDERSTAND THE RULES OF PUNCTUATION

Over the years, the teaching of punctuation has suffered some bad press. The SPaG (spelling, punctuation and grammar) lesson was often frowned on because it was seen as lazy. In some eyes, if it isn't active, physical or flamboyant then it isn't teaching. A teacher simply pulls out a grammar textbook and students proceed to complete the task. Where was the teacher acting out at the front of the class? Where was the card sort? The essentials were lost in entertainment pretending to be teaching. Punctuation got a rough deal. It wasn't sexy. Yes, people might have a penchant for semicolons or colons because they appear as if they might be difficult. But, you wouldn't see teachers planning a lesson on comma usage if they wanted it to be 'outstanding'.

Punctuation, love it or hate it, is an integral part of writing and communication. We all know how a comma in the wrong place makes it sound like someone is going to eat their granny, but there is something important about learning the function of pieces of punctuation, or even how they can have multiple functions. Without this level of precision, we end up just telling students to chuck in an exclamation mark because Ros Wilson's 'Punctuation Pyramid' tells us it's better than a comma.[7] Or just use a comma when there is a pause. Punctuation has been simplified, neglected and misused.

We have even got to the stage where we have endless battles between the pro- and anti-teaching-grammar camps on Twitter. Personally, I think you need a healthy balance of both explicit grammar teaching and implicit learning through reading. They go hand in hand, not arm against arm. Learning what a conditional sentence[8] is will not instantaneously make you the greatest writer, but it will help you to notice the different ways writers use it. Later, you will be able to adopt it in your own writing. I don't agree with the vocal (mainly children's) writers who spout how the learning of grammar rules is actually detrimental to expression. Some of our greatest Victorian writers had the most rigid and explicit grammar teaching and they turned out alright. To an extent, English teaching has always been a battle between order and chaos – or

---

7 See http://www.andrelleducation.com/big-writing/.
8 A conditional sentence is a complex sentence often made from two clauses exploring the impact of a certain condition/context/scenario. One clause contains a condition: 'If I am late' and the other an outcome or solution: 'you can start making tea.'

simply, rules and freedom. We want students to be creative, but we also want them to follow the rules of language. It is far better for this to happen from a place of knowledge rather than by happenstance, serendipity and ignorance.

Grammar is like the rules behind a game. You could still play without them, but you wouldn't do it properly and chaos would ensue. Yeah, you might score a goal, but how do you know what a goal is, or what skill and finesse look like. You'll most likely be disqualified in any case because you didn't follow the rules. When you have the rules clear in your head, you can use them to your advantage, use them to find the shortcuts and, ultimately, to win. Plus, rules help narrow the parameters. There is less chaos and fewer variables, so what you effectively work on is a narrow band of skills.

There's a glut of people in society, often famous writers, who argue that they weren't explicitly taught grammar but look at how successful they are. A group of people who seem to have had an education on a *Lord of the Flies* style island devoid of adult supervision and rules. Like the boys in William Golding's *Lord of the Flies*, it seems idyllic and fun, but I don't think Piggy would agree. Explicit teaching of grammar ensures that students, like Piggy, are not let down and have a chance to succeed.

It is our job to help our students master the rules of writing, and those jobs may be forfeited if Tiny Tim decides to write his story without any punctuation because he wants to symbolise the way the education system has stymied his creativity. Yes, it might be lovely and beautiful that a student can express his ideas through a rhyming couplet, but if that student can't write a competent letter of application then the couplet is unlikely to be of much use. There is a moral dimension to grammar. We want students to better themselves and understanding grammar is one way to do that. All too often, those protesting about explicit grammar teaching are not interacting with students day in, day out. So what would they know?

Take the simple exclamation mark: a mark that editors hate and that has been abused for decades. In lessons, it is used with gleeful abandon to show shock. But doesn't it have another purpose? To show disgust? To show disbelief? To show surprise? Young writers overuse the exclamation mark because social media has made it acceptable.

What is that!

I am not going to touch it!

Not again!

The exclamation mark is used for different effects. The function is the same, yet the purpose is different. Teach the function of the punctuation, then explore its purpose. We know that single inverted commas are used to separate words from the original text, yet the purpose of inverted commas can also be to show sarcasm, humour, exaggeration, shock, disgust, etc.

I often get students to use punctuation with purpose. Well, effect really, because I blur the two together. Telling students to use different pieces from the 'Punctuation Pyramid' is helpful to develop variety, but it is pretty useless when you are trying to use punctuation to any sophisticated level. Therefore, I get students to use punctuation with a particular effect in mind.

Use inverted commas to be sarcastic.

The dress was incredibly 'fashionable'.

Use ellipses to show you have forgotten something.

I walked down the stairs thinking about something to do with ... with ... something I couldn't remember.

Use a colon for dramatic effect by referring back to something that was hinted at before.

The room was empty apart from a dark figure: a statue whose eyes looked directly at me and blinked.

Use two dashes to add a parenthetical comment and change the tone of the writing.

The journey back home had been surprisingly quiet – I later realised I had forgotten to put the baby in the car when I left the shopping centre – as I plodded through my daily routine.

Always link punctuation to effect and to function. Students need to be explicitly taught these functions. We want students to write with clear purpose and this needs to be drip-fed to them all the time. Punctuation has a job and an effect.

5. LISTS, LISTS, LISTS

I believe it is better to teach one thing really well than lots of things badly. Over the years, acronyms have sprouted up to try to teach/force decent writing to/onto students. They have always, in my opinion, ended up with students trying to cram absolutely everything into one sentence or paragraph. One such example was AFOREST (as we saw, a simple acronym to ensure students use alliteration, facts, opinions, rhetorical questions, emotive language, statistics and tone, not much appreciated by examiners). It reduced writing to a series of bolt-on techniques. Through such a prism, a good piece of writing will cycle through a predetermined list of techniques. Writers don't work like this, of course. You can't imagine Jane Austen agonising over the fact that she hasn't used a rhetorical question in a paragraph. Yet English teachers use this approach to engineer Frankenstein's monster in writing.

Teaching often leads to conceptual reduction rather than clarification. I'm a big believer in teaching something in great detail and making students masters of that aspect. Over the year, we will keep coming back to things previously taught. Instead of repeating the reductive muddle of AFOREST, I ask students to remind me of variations, for instance, of using a list in a sentence. In my experience, students can write far more effectively by using lists than through employing some daft acronym.

Structurally, there are three main places to use a list in a sentence: at the start, in the middle and at the end.

---

1   *Coffee, Twitter and music keep me sane.*

2   *I wonder how I ever coped without video games, TV and the Internet as a child living in Wales.*

3   *Wales has a historic tradition of singing, playing rugby and cwtching.*[9]

Teaching students to write using lists is like going back to the beginning. The problem with lists is that they are generally used as a simple functional device: 'I need to list the objects I placed in my bag.' Students don't often see them as tools with which we can affect style or meaning.

A list at the start of a sentence can help to bamboozle a reader by linking odd combinations of words.

A brick, a carrot and a notepad are the things I regularly carry in my handbag.

A list at the end of a sentence can create a sense of drama.

The day was interesting: it featured fun, laughter and death.

---

9   This is a big Welsh cuddle.

A list in an unusual or particular place can create a sense of expectation. In horror stories and ghost stories, the power of suggestion is incredibly effective. The first noise is something harmless. The second noise is harmless too. By the time we get to the third noise, we think it is harmless but, in fact, it is a mass murderer getting ready to add to his list of victims. This 'rule of three' can be used to great effect in stories.

On the cold, dark and lonely moor nestled a cold, dark, lonely house where a woman sat in a window with cold, dark and lonely thoughts and murder on her mind.

The man's empty, cold and narrow eyes followed the people and his mind too was empty, cold and narrow, but the thing in his hands wasn't empty: it was cold and narrow.

Lists aren't just affected by where you place them in a sentence but also by what you list.

Now, my shopping bag ordinarily contains eggs, flour and milk. My annoyance, anger and humiliation became evident when I returned home to see I'd (incorrectly, mistakenly and stupidly) forgotten to buy wine – the most important ingredient for all meals. Well, my meals, anyway.

Listing different parts of speech (or other varieties of abstraction) can produce some interesting effects. Consider the effect created by the following.

A list of emotions. *Anger, frustration and fury were all he felt at that time.*

A list of verbs. *The train shuddered, rocked, tilted and jolted over the tracks.*

A list of adverbs. *He typed the email furiously, frantically, fitfully.*

A list of prepositions. *The balls flew near, over and beneath the people seated on their chairs.*

A list of pronouns. *She couldn't decide if it was her, him or them to blame for the accident.*

A list of words with the same prefix. *She felt unimportant, unnecessary, uninvited and unwanted at the party.*

A list of words with the same suffix. *The tree was fruitless, hopeless and meaningless.*

A list of similes. *Time moved slowly like a lazy, tired animal, like it had no care in the world, like a petulant child instructed to tidy its room.*

A list of colours. *The flowers' greens, light blues and aggressive reds camouflaged the creatures hiding among the petals.*

A list of sounds. *The wheels of the car crunched, shattered and scratched the pieces of glass.*

I could go on. There are so many variables. Yet we rarely teach students to experiment and play with lists. Students could consider how many items they might put in a list, or they could consider the order. The beauty of lists is that they are not limited to writing. Lists have a valuable benefit for analysis. They can highlight complexity and multiple meanings. 'The article persuades, shocks and advises us of the dangers of smoking.' A sentence like this shows us that the student understands that the text has a number of purposes. If the student lists those purposes in the order in which they appear in the text, then the student will be commenting on the structure as well as the purpose.

A list of the writer's purpose/message. *Shakespeare's* Much Ado About Nothing *highlights how men view love, how easily they damage relationships and how they struggle to articulate and manage their feelings.*

A list of the reader's/audience's feelings. *The audience respects, idolises and fears Othello at the start of the play.*

A list of words to describe the text/character. *Macbeth's insecurity, naïvety and inconsistency combine to fuel his downfall.*

A list of techniques. *The use of alliteration, words associated with pain and the word 'danger' combine to create a sense of fear as the poet expresses the reality of the soldier's fate.*

The list of possibilities is endless, infinite and continuous.

6. MODEL AND READ ALOUD

I write in almost every lesson. I think it is important that students see me writing. I set students off to write and I have a go myself while they are doing it, asking myself the entirely reasonable question: can I do what I am expecting students to do? My early years of teaching were spent setting students off to write and then waiting at the front to see what they would produce, wondering how much work I'd have to mark or what I'd have for tea. Like an expectant father, I'd pace the classroom. Usually, the arrival was met with tears but not of joy.

Now, I do the same task as them. And, as I am sharing their experience, I am able to ask questions like:

- Who else found it difficult to start?

- Did anybody else manage to use a rhetorical question? (What's that? You struggled, Jane? Never mind.)

- Anybody else struggle to fit that word in?

There are few things more powerful than a shared experience in learning. Years down the line, every student can remember the time a wasp got into the classroom and the time Bill vomited over the front row of desks. A shared experience easily becomes a shared memory as we constantly remind each other of it. The other advantage of sharing the experience is that students can see what a good example looks like and, even more importantly, how you write.

Able students are great, but they can give others a misguided idea of how easy it is to achieve success. There will always be students who can quickly produce superb pieces of work with little apparent effort. Other students will see them as something to aspire to: that's why some boys race to finish first because that's what 'brighter' students seem to do. Me tapping away on the board helps students to see the pace at which I write, which is quite slow. It also allows them to steal or borrow ideas, words or phrases for their own writing. Speed of writing is needed in the final exams, but not necessarily in the years leading up to them. I set the pace for the completion of the task.

The other advantage of having a clear, visual example is as a point of reference. I love saying to students, when we have finished, 'Who wrote it like I did? Who didn't?' At that point, you learn about the different possibilities on offer. The students learn that there is more than one way to approach the task. Also, they can see the humour in my writing. I love being playful and I model this to the students. Can I write a paragraph without the word 'the'? Can I describe a setting without mentioning anything visual? Can I reference the head teacher without the class knowing?

At this point, I get a chance to read students' work out loud. This, I feel, is a neglected aspect. We get students to read out their own work and that is commendable, but it lacks the life and power of the teacher doing so. I can use my delivery to turn the most turgid, clunking prose into something rather more atmospheric. I love the drama of reading out a student's writing and, whether it be a letter or a piece of creative writing, I am modelling how the text *might* be received and experienced. The voice of the writing is reflected in how I speak. I will pause for emphasis, speed things up, slow things down. All the time, I'm modelling the way the text is communicating to the reader. Every text is a performance. Teach students that writing is a performance and it becomes more interesting.

Over the years, this has been incredibly powerful as bright boys, especially, try to build up the humour and explore different ways of creating an effect. I always find one student is willing to push the boundaries to try and outsmart me. For a whole year, one played a cat and mouse game with me. We both had fun and the class did too because we were writing for an audience – each other. The class couldn't wait to see how the student had ridiculed and belittled me. I am 5 foot 5. There was a theme.

7. LOTS OF WRITING – THE 200 WORD CHALLENGE

I've changed the way I view writing over the years, and now think there isn't enough of it in schools. Students don't write enough in English or in other subjects. There's a simple reason for this: the expectation that every piece of work should be marked in depth. Senior leaders have propelled this expectation to the extent that, in some schools, teachers avoid extended writing so that they don't have to mark so much. This has caused a problem. The fear of being judged by an outsider for not marking work has changed the balance in the classroom. The fear is a genuine one, but it should be addressed by any good senior leader. The students should be working harder than the teacher. Fact! An exercise book should be full of work. That's what I want to see. If not, what have you been teaching and what has the student been learning? If we want students to be better writers, we need them to improve their fluency – and that only comes with constant writing.

In English, our units of work are planned around using a particular style termed 'transactional writing'. We spend whole terms analysing how and preparing to write in such styles, but the creativity, fun and enjoyment are leeched out when you are five weeks into term and now you get to write your very own letter to a charity. The immediacy of writing is often neglected. You either have wishy-washy musings about a character's feelings in a play or you have a rigid style that students must emulate otherwise they have failed to understand the text type.

In my school, we've changed the way we view writing. We've made it a weekly thing. In the last lesson of the week, we get students to write a piece of fiction or non-fiction. Each week is a different style and a surprise. Rather than get students to produce one piece of extended writing a term, we get them to produce multiple stylistically different smaller pieces. They write more and, to be honest, what they produce now is more creative.

We followed a process very similar to the various writing challenges used in primary schools. First, we give the students a PowerPoint slide with the following information:

Persuade teachers that you are the best student in the school

You must include the following:

- A link to a historical event.
- A line from a famous song.
- A quote from a well-known speech.
- A simile.
- A fact.

You must include the following word in your writing:

Indisputable: it is true and nobody can argue with the fact. As in, *Mrs Jones' cooking is indisputably good.*

Students then write for twenty-five minutes, aiming to produce at least 200 words. There are no interruptions. Students are expected to write without asking questions so they can build up their independence. If the text or task is particularly challenging, the teacher might clarify or reteach an aspect. During the writing, I will mark ten students' work and help them.

For the second half of the lesson, students peer assess using the following format:

Peer assessment

1   Highlight and label the following: a link to a historical event, a line from a famous song, a quote from a well-known speech, a simile, a fact.

2   Circle any errors.

3   Write down what they need to do to improve the content/structure/writing.

4   Sign and date it.

Finally, I get students to respond to the peer assessment with this:

Correct each circled mistake and write a quick explanation of the mistake – spelling/I missed a letter/I forgot a comma.

In the final few minutes, I read out some of the best examples. If there is a really good one, I photocopy it for the next class so it can inspire and direct them.

Yes, this is the old kind of composition task that was commonplace many years ago, but it worked very well for both teachers and students. Teachers were happy because lessons were easily planned, and it helped revise techniques from other areas of the curriculum. Boys were happy because it was immediate, quick and gave them the freedom to use humour. Girls liked it because they could be more creative and because the previous teaching of writing was fairly restrictive. The students' writing has improved but, more importantly, their voices have developed through writing more. And it's not the same students producing the best pieces all the time. Who knew Lucy could be so sardonic and witty in her writing?

Students look forward to the 200 Word Challenge now. It's a chance to be creative, to be surprised by the task, to experiment. We love playful and witty writers, yet we often don't create the environment for students to be as creative as they might be. The manacles need to come off sometimes. Just get students to write more. When they are writing, they are thinking. And that is what we want.

Chapter 3
HOW TO TEACH NOVELS

Sadly, over the years, there's been a huge decrease in the number of schools teaching novels in full. The demands and pressures of exams has meant that the experience has been narrowed and compartmentalised and novels reduced to key extracts. My feeling is that students should experience as many novels as possible, and it is the role of the English department to ensure they do just that.

The key word in the above paragraph is 'experience', because that is what a novel is. The danger can be in placing too much emphasis on making it about enjoyment and fun. By reading a novel, students experience the situations the characters live through. A different world. A different time. If we teach them that reading is solely about enjoyment, we neglect an integral part of the experience. By reading a novel, you get a feel for and learn from a person who is not you, who is different. Make it about enjoyment and you reduce a complex experience to a star rating. What would you give that chapter out of five?

I have watched the approach to novels change and, probably more importantly, the books selected have also undergone a profound shift. As a child in the eighties, I read and was taught about social issues: books explored in the classroom tended to have an agenda. In the nineties and noughties, they tended to focus on plot rather than issues. They'd be sparsely written, but they'd have a good story. I tend to prefer complex books and something with a bit of bite, something political, something meaty and adult to work with, something with bigger ideas, something that doesn't talk down to children. My favourite ones to teach are:

Charles Dickens' *Great Expectations* and *Oliver Twist*

Charlotte Brontë's *Jane Eyre*

George Orwell's *Animal Farm*

Robert Louis Stevenson's *Treasure Island*

William Golding's *Lord of the Flies*

I like teaching them for several reasons, but mainly because they teach the lesson themselves. Pick up any of these books and you can always find something interesting and meaningful to say about the way in which they're written. Take a lot of modern class readers and you really have to struggle. These books are classics for a reason.

Another reason why the selection of titles is important is, again, about experience. Students would not necessarily gravitate towards these books unless they have particularly pushy parents or a desire to read everything, so these books open their eyes to a new realm. I am always surprised when teachers are all for reading Shakespeare yet bemoan the use of classics as they don't speak or appeal to students. I go back to the point I made at the start of this book: it is the teacher's job to make texts relevant. If you select a book on the basis of interest, then you are being lazy. Taking the route of least resistance is easy. I could certainly teach lessons on films, TV shows and computer games. Would that make them better writers? No. A teacher made *Jane Eyre* relevant to me. And that teacher became more relevant by their use of the book. I connected with the book and, as the teacher was part of that process, with them.

We like to think we know best: the 'I was a teenager once and so therefore know what teenagers like' idea. Human beings are complex and have complex interests. You can never predict what a student will like or engage with emotionally or intellectually. I'd say that we are in danger of insulting students and reinforcing negative stereotypes if we pick texts to suit them rather than simply going for effective, interesting and intellectually stimulating books. Picking a book because it has blood, death and violence for the boys will create a limited cycle of experience. No one style of film, literature or music pleases everybody. We each have such a variety of interests that if you tried to pick something to suit everyone you'd have a mighty struggle. So just pick a challenging book and see what interests the students. Often you'll find it isn't what you expected.

The other thing to draw on is the magic of reading. It has saved me planning lessons. It has saved the behaviour of a class. Read a novel and the class can become hypnotised; quiet, attentive and focused. Why wouldn't you repeat that again and again? Why would you not have whole lessons dedicated to reading?

There has never been a better time to be a book lover. Books are brilliantly presented nowadays and there are entire publishing imprints geared towards young people, but we have to build a love for and a culture of reading. There is a problem with students' concentration, and books are the remedy. The level of concentration needed to read a book is intense, yet we are reading shorter and shorter extracts because we fear that reading isn't learning. I would dare to say that English departments are pioneers in building concentration. I will spend acres of time reading with a class because I am building up their concentration and their ability to focus. Will they not need this in the exam?

1. KNOWLEDGE IS EVERYTHING – HISTORY

There's an interesting debate around reading in class. Do you reveal the plot and then read the novel? Or do you let the plot unfold over time? It is a hard decision to make, but it is an important one.

There are several elements to cover when studying a novel: plot, character, language, themes and structure. And they tend to follow this order of complexity. Plot, unless it is a Shakespeare play or a whodunnit, is usually the easiest to grasp. It is hard to talk effectively about structure and themes when a student isn't secure on the plot and characters. You see this when students constantly ask who the characters are or who, in their writing, insist on retelling the plot. They do this to establish the basics. If you let the plot unfold, then you are constantly starting at zero and working through those comprehension elements. What happened? What has changed with the characters? What is interesting about how it is written?

The popularity of John Steinbeck's *Of Mice and Men* is, in part, due to its easily distinguished and recognisable characters: the one with curly hair, the one with a stump for a hand and a smelly dog: the one everybody loves and admires. Harper Lee's superior (in my opinion) *To Kill a Mockingbird* isn't as popular as it has a wider community of characters. For years, I hid Lennie and George's fate in *Of Mice and Men* because I was trying to hold on to the personal experience the students have when encountering a book for the first time. The sad thing is that reading in the classroom is a collective experience, so you can guarantee that someone in 'the collective' will announce loudly that George kills Lennie, or will relish whispering it to their neighbour who, in turn, will pass it around like classroom gossip.

We are more interested in the way the book is written than the plot. How many exams ask students to retell the story in their own words? When looking at how a novel is written, you need to know the plot really well. But only in a murder mystery is the ending the most important thing. All other stories are about the journey rather than the destination.

Give students the plot from the start. Tell them loosely what happens. The rise of the knowledge organiser has helped with this element (see pages 80–83).

Then, when they know the plot of the story, they can see the following when reading:

- How Steinbeck foreshadows the fate of the characters.
- How Steinbeck makes us like the characters, especially Lennie, so we feel attached to them and shocked at the ending.
- How Steinbeck sets up the characters as clear goodies and baddies.
- How Steinbeck builds up and destroys hope.

Reveal the story one chapter at a time and you are less likely to get to that high level of insight because your time is spent looking at the plot and the characters (focusing on the 'what' rather than the 'how'). Watch a decent film. You get caught up in the plot, and you fail to see the beautiful and subtle use of lighting and colour. It is usually only on the second or third viewing that you pick up these nuances. Focus on the plot and you might as well be an entertainer. I have listened to teachers enthuse about whole classes crying at the death of Lennie and have been a little jealous that they managed to prevent students from finding out spoilers.

An important part of the reading experience is understanding the historical context. Too often we look through the culturally conditioned eyes of an adult. I have read lots of books, so it is easy to forget that I pick up the subtle things writers do to create a world. Plus, as an adult reader, I have lots of points of reference. I might have watched a film set at the time or read a book that explores the period. Students have more limited frames of reference. I can't guarantee that every student has watched *Oliver!*, so when teaching a Victorian novel I have to start by assuming that their slate is more or less blank. Take the following points I provide when reading *A Christmas Carol*:

A Christmas Carol: 1843, historical context

- The Industrial Revolution allowed the rich to exploit the poor and thus become richer.
- The industries tended to be located near major cities so people migrated from rural to urban areas seeking jobs.
- There was not enough space to accommodate the influx of people so settlements became overcrowded.
- Particular areas of overcrowding were referred to as slums.
- Increased rates of diseases and illnesses occurred as a result of overcrowding and poor sanitation.
- Life expectancy was low and infant mortality high in the lower classes, so it was common for families to be large.

I am not only teaching them the story but the world it inhabits, so they understand the novel better. Stories are about world building. Some are closer to our own world than others, but we have to make that clear. A science fiction story might build a barely recognisable world, but the teacher needs to help deconstruct a world that was written with a contemporary readership, rather than our students, in mind; this can appear just as unfamiliar.

After giving students these statements, I ask them what they think the Victorians' attitudes or feelings towards death or childhood were. The facts themselves are limited points of understanding. Context isn't just about facts; it's about ideas. Facts become meaningful when attached to the texts studied. When reading *Great Expectations* and *A Christmas Carol*, students are always shocked by the treatment of infant mortality because current rates are so relatively low as to be, in their eyes, nigh on non-existent and so not a factor to consider. I have had students imply that Pip's parents were overly randy rather than address the fact that the chances of a child living

Year 9 knowledge organiser: *Of Mice and Men*

Year 9 Knowledge Organiser – *Of Mice and Men*		
Of Mice and Men is a bleak tale of two migrant workers; the novel suggests that in order for life to be meaningful, it must contain hopes and dreams, even if they are unachievable.		
Context	Characters	
The Great Depression took place following the Wall Street Crash in October 1929 and affected the world's economy. Wall Street is a street in New York City, where many financial firms are based, and the term Wall Street is used to describe the American financial sector. The Wall Street Crash happened as a result of the following factors: • many normal Americans had started investing in the stock exchange and were borrowing money in order to do so • stock prices rose unsustainably And then stock owners all attempted to sell shares at the same time (Black Tuesday). Other actions that contributed included: too many goods being made while not enough were being bought, and food prices were dropping, affecting farmers' incomes. Following the Wall Street Crash, the USA recalled the huge loans that it had made to several European countries, meaning that the European economy was also affected by the crash.	George: Lennie's closest friend, George is protective of Lennie and loyal towards him, claiming Lennie stops him from getting mean. However, George can sometimes lack patience with Lennie's optimism. Curley: an insecure, violent man who actively looks for violence or opportunities to prove his worth. Incredibly possessive of his wife, Curley seems to pick fights to compensate for his lack of size.	Lennie: naïve, immensely strong and gentle, Lennie has a mental disability that means he is solely reliant upon George. As a result, Lennie is the focus of Curley's cruelty. Curley's wife: flirtatious and lonely, Curley's wife is presented as a danger to the other men because of the consequences if Curley suspects that they have interacted with her. She shares her lost dreams with Lennie, emphasising her lack of companionship.

Slim: self-assured and respected, Slim is the calm, quiet authority of the men at the ranch. He understands George and Lennie's friendship but even he cannot protect others.

Crooks: cynical and yet to an extent a believer in the American Dream, stable manager and the only black migrant worker on the farm. As a result of this, he sleeps in the stables, segregated from the other men.

Candy: the oldest worker, Candy is a crippled handyman with a feeble dog. Broken by life, Candy is desperate to believe in a dream or plan. He offers to help George and Lennie by cashing in his life savings to help them buy a farm.

The American Dream is written into the Declaration of Independence: 'life, liberty, and the pursuit of happiness'. Lennie and George's dream of owning a farm and living off the 'fatta the lan' symbolises this dream. *Of Mice and Men* shows that for poor migrant workers during the Depression, the American Dream became an illusion and a trap.

John Steinbeck was an American writer (1902–1968) who was born in Salinas, where the novella is set. He often wrote stories as morality tales or allegories, that attempted to criticise or consider the social problems presented by the Great Depression or the struggles of particular groups that suffered segregation.
His other notable works include *The Grapes of Wrath*, *The Pearl* and *East of Eden*.

Plot – the action of the novella takes place over four days.

1. George and Lennie camp in the brush by a pool, the night before starting new jobs as ranch hands. George finds Lennie stroking a dead mouse in his pocket. He complains that caring for Lennie prevents him from living a freer life. We find out that Lennie's innocent petting of a girl's dress led to them losing their last jobs in Weed. However, when they talk about their dream of getting a piece of land together, we know that they really do depend on each other.

2. When they arrive at the ranch in the morning, George and Lennie are shown around by old Candy. They meet their boss and, later, his son, Curley – George is suspicious of Curley's manner and warns Lennie to stay away from him.

3. Later that evening, George tells Slim about why he and Lennie travel together and more about what happened in Weed. The men talk about Candy's ancient dog, which is tired and ill. Carlson shoots it, as an act of kindness. George tells Candy about their dream of getting a piece of land and Candy eagerly offers to join them – he has capital, so they could make it happen almost immediately. Curley provokes Lennie into a fight, which ends with Lennie severely injuring Curley's hand.

4. Crooks is alone in his room when Lennie joins him. They talk about land – Crooks is sceptical, not believing that George and Lennie are going to achieve what so many other men he's known have failed to do, and get land of their own. Yet when Candy happens to come in as well, Crooks is convinced and asks to be in on it too. Curley's wife arrives. She threatens Crooks and an argument develops. Crooks realises he can never really be part of George, Lennie and Candy's plan.

5. Next afternoon, Lennie accidentally kills the puppy that Slim had given him by petting it too much. He's sad. Curley's wife finds him and starts talking very openly about her feelings. She invites Lennie to stroke her soft hair, but he does it so strongly she panics and he ends up killing her too. He runs away to hide, as George has told him.

   Candy finds the body and tells George. They tell the other men – Curley wants revenge.

6. Lennie hides in the brush by the pool. He dreams of his Aunt Clara and the rabbits he will tend when he and George get their land.

   George finds Lennie and talks reassuringly to him about the little place they will have together – then shoots him with Carlson's gun.

   When the other men find George, they assume he shot Lennie in self-defence. Only Slim understands what George did and why.

Themes	Hopes and dreams, loneliness and companionship, brutality and dignity	Key vocabulary	
			Disengaged
			Hierarchy
			Derogatory
			Pugnacious
			Isolation
			Motif
			Prejudice
			Segregation
			Microcosm
			Dustbowl
			Cyclical narrative

Source: Kat Howard

to adulthood were significantly lower in Victorian times. For us it might be obvious, but for students it is alien.

I list contextual facts and then get students to empathise by asking how they'd feel if this was their reality. We are building relevance. The historical context might be alien, but the issues are often universal. Sometimes, I will add the notion of 'rules'. Based on these facts, what were the rules of life then? Under the contextual facts, there is always a form of etiquette: a code of behaviour or rules for life. They might be subtle, but they are there and they are constantly changing. We don't want students to spout endless facts; instead, we want something more thoughtful, deeper. If you were living in this world (or time), what would affect your thinking? How would you think? Using our facts on *A Christmas Carol,* a student could say something along the lines of, 'If you are poor, you would expect to face constant challenges and that your social position and quality of life would never improve while you remain poor.'

I constantly keep referring to the rules of a specific historical period. You might refer to it as the code of conduct, the rules of behaviour or social etiquette, but it all amounts to the same thing: the hidden rules that govern the way we behave.

2. POETIC STRUCTURE

Decluttering is helpful when getting students to see the explicit choices a writer makes. I do this by simply reducing the text so that it looks like poetry.

---

fog and frost hung

about the black old gateway of the house

a knocker

impenetrable shadow

dismal light

like a bad lobster in a dark cellar

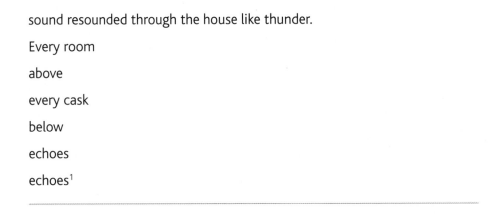

sound resounded through the house like thunder.

Every room

above

every cask

below

echoes

echoes[1]

As a rule, I never add any words. I will only ever remove and then attempt to shape meaning by using a new line or indenting lines. What this does is help students to analyse the text more effectively by focusing on the words in finer detail. One of the big problems students have when analysing a prose text is the volume of information. They are simply swamped, and that's why they tend to list ideas and techniques. But English is never about the number of observations but the quality of the response.

Some of things students might notice about the 'poetrified' extract from *A Christmas Carol* include:

- The sense of size of the building is conveyed by its 'echo' and the use of 'above' and 'below'.

- The unpleasant and unwelcoming atmosphere – 'impenetrable', 'dismal', 'thunder'.

- The sense of loneliness conveyed through the use of the lobster imagery and the echoes.

- The sense of wealth with the use of the word 'every'.

We then look at the full text and highlight the aspects we've identified in the poetic version. It allows them to see what is missing and if I have misinterpreted any aspect. The more we get students to engage with and interrogate the text, the better.

---

1   Dickens, *A Christmas Carol*, p. 21.

A further variation on this theme is 'blackout poetry'. Check it out on the Internet. Put simply, a student takes a page of text and blacks out words so the remaining ones form a poem. This tackles the idea from the opposite perspective. And we can get students to do the work we might otherwise be doing on a Sunday.

3. BE CLEAR ABOUT THE WRITER'S STYLE

When we introduce Shakespeare, we tend to prepare students for his style of writing. Yet we often don't prepare them for other writers' styles. I'll admit that the opening chapter is often a struggle for me. Not because of the plot, characters or ideas, but because I am having to get used to the *style* of the writing. It takes my brain a bit of time to do this, and I suspect I am not alone in being disorientated sometimes. It is probably why you have to prise *Diary of a Wimpy Kid* or Jacqueline Wilson's books from students' hands. They are comfortable, consistent and relatable. We get hooked on how people write.

I am clear from the start about style, and I explicitly tell students what is unique about the way the writer has written a book. It might be consistent throughout their work, or particular to one book; we all like to experiment.

Take William Golding's *Lord of the Flies*. These are the things I'd make explicit about the style:

- There are large descriptions of the setting.
- Golding emphasises the way the setting looks rather than the way the characters look.
- Characters are presented through their dialogue.
- There is more dialogue than description and action.
- The dialogue isn't always clear and the speaker is often ambiguous.

Of course, I could be more precise and often I am, depending on the class. What I'm doing is helping to reduce the disorientating effect and getting students to see what is unique about the way in which the text is written. Again, the writer has made choices. Why focus more on dialogue than characters? Is it simply because they are all so similar? Also, when students have these features of style clear in their heads, you can then explore when the writer deviates from it. Why doesn't Golding use dialogue at this point?

When writers have a large body of work, it's helpful to look at how texts are consistent with the rest. Is it typical of the writer? Is it unusual? When students have an idea of the 'basic style model' the writer uses, you can then explore the relationship between the various elements. It can be discussed through the use of percentages, pie charts or graphs. The chapter is 70% dialogue, 10% setting and 20% action. The emphasis on dialogue could suggest that the chapter is focusing on relationships.

Take Dickens. We teach students to be aware of several aspects of his style. Style includes content, techniques and themes.

Content

- Young male protagonists growing up.
- Clearly defined good and bad characters.
- Comical characters.
- Melodramatic events.

Techniques

- Exaggeration/Hyperbole.
- Similes.
- Personification.
- Repetition.
- Lists.
- Triplets.
- Contrasts.

- (Intrusive/Omniscient) Narrative voice.

- Themes.

Themes

We also use pictograms and images to explore and secure knowledge of themes. 'Dual coding' – the theory of which was first expounded in the early 1970s by Allan Paivio – is a particularly powerful way to help students retain knowledge.[2] It works on the principle of using visual and verbal channels of communication together to aid learning, rather than just focusing on one channel over another. We use it to help students learn, memorise and recall key ideas and techniques. We use a picture to represent a theme, and refer to it repeatedly in explanations, questioning and discussion. In subsequent lessons, we use the image as the starting point. Students seem to retain things better using the combination of symbols and explanations.

This body of knowledge is our starting point. Look at the difference between these two statements:

1   The writer uses repetition in the description of the character.

2   Consistent with his typical style, the writer uses repetition in the description of the character.

---

2   See https://plato.stanford.edu/entries/mental-imagery/theories-memory.html.

Seeing what makes and breaks a pattern is a skill we can promote in students. Going back to the aspects of a novel, themes and structure are all about how things are connected. We want to see the intent behind the masterpiece. We can't rely on spotting techniques and narrowing our focus onto small sections. You wouldn't look at a single brushstroke in a painting; instead you'd look at the combination. We need to do the same with writing.

4. FEELINGS

It can be hard for students to articulate their reaction to a novel. I wish I had a pound for every student who's told me that a writer made a choice for the simple reason of making the reader read on. This implies that there are writers who want to do the opposite.

We do need to be open with feelings in the classroom, and especially those that students might not be comfortable expressing. Take confusion. We hear about it, but don't regularly embrace it with students. Look at the text again: where are you confused? Students tend to oscillate between excitement and boredom. Texts are reduced to 'exciting' or 'boring' very quickly, so it is our job to explicitly talk about the wealth of emotions they can elicit. We must add to students' repertoire and their, possibly quite limited, expressive vocabulary.

Teach emotions

Teach students emotions as you go along. Take 'apathy' or 'indifference'; students can bring these emotions to their discussion of texts. The teacher might introduce these words by using them in their questioning. Does anybody feel indifference towards the character here? Does anybody get the feeling of apathy from the minor characters? If we want emotions to be part of students' written analysis, we must make them part of the classroom dialogue. If we allow 'exciting' and 'boring' to dominate, we are narrowing the quality of the conversation. We miss out on their anxiety when a character is close to making a mistake. We ignore their jubilation when a character accepts a marriage proposal. We deny our fear when a character gets locked in a room with a murderer.

I find some of the following techniques useful when developing students' knowledge of more complex emotional responses:

- Repeat the word so many times in so many different contexts that it becomes a catchphrase.
- Get students to write a story in which a character experiences that emotion.
- Compare emotions. What is the difference between boredom and apathy?
- Use music. What are you meant to feel when you listen to this part of a song?

It could be argued that social media has simplified our emotional reactions: we either 'like' or 'dislike' something, everything. My own teenage years were made difficult by my inability to express emotion in any articulate manner. I was a door slammer. That was how I communicated with my family. One slam for annoyance. Two for fury. Young people need the tools to express themselves emotionally so that they do not, like I did, have to resort to the brutality of the physical – and, for that, they need a teacher who will model the language to express such feelings.

Read with emotion

Rather than zooming in on a text and its meaning, just get students to write down what they feel or think as they read. More importantly, get them to highlight the parts where those feelings change. Nobody can maintain boredom for a whole text. But don't challenge me on that one!

Write with emotion

Teaching a novel is also a good opportunity to practise creative writing. Reading a class reader is a long-term exposure to one particular style of writing and an opportunity to incorporate what the writer does into students' own writing. Osmosis happens when students write near a text they have been reading. They pick up the gimmicks, the turns of phrase, the approaches, the vocabulary and the syntax of the writer. The best writers steal ideas and we need to teach students to steal things. Imagine how difficult it would be if everything you write had to be fresh, new and unlike anything anyone has written.

The problem students have when they write prose fiction is that they write for themselves; unlike novelists, who know how to write for their readership – well, maybe not all novelists. They create stories with one emotion. That's why boys tend to have zombies and explosions and death in the first paragraph. Teach students to structure their writing around emotions instead. That's why a novel or an extract from a novel is such a great starting point. Students can see how the emotions change paragraph by paragraph and then attempt to replicate it.

Paragraph 1 – anger

Paragraph 2 – bliss

Paragraph 3 – disappointment

Paragraph 4 – contentment

From a novel-reading perspective, seeing how and what makes the emotion change in a section is an incredibly useful way to understand what is going on in a story. This works with non-fiction too.

Be clear about the emotional impact of a choice

Let's go back to a question from the start of this book and reword it:

What is the emotional reason for Charles Dickens using Oliver Twist instead of Olivia Twist?

A simple question like this might lead us to even more interesting and possibly difficult questions in a time of greater equality.

Would our emotions towards Oliver be different if he were female?

Does Dickens have a specific reason for making Oliver male rather than female? Does the use of a male protagonist in Victorian England give a different perspective than a female protagonist would?

Of course, Dickens is concerned with highlighting the plight of the poor in Victorian society and Oliver Twist is a device used to make us see how the abuse is systematic and prevalent. Girls living in poverty were equally mistreated, so there isn't a clear reason for the choice. However, is there an emotional dimension? Are our natural 'maternal' or 'paternal' instincts and desires to protect a child stronger towards girls than boys? Victorian melodrama favoured the gender imbalance of a helpless female at the mercy of a strong male figure. However, a man selling a young girl could suggest ideas of prostitution and exploitation, so could Dickens be explicitly avoiding this unpleasant connotation by selecting a boy? Is he showing us that poverty rather than gender creates the victims?

Explore the emotional impact of a writer's choices. Why give Lennie learning difficulties yet make him physically able? More interestingly, how would our emotions change towards Lennie if his difficulties were physical? Readers identify with certain characters: Steinbeck, I think, puts the reader in the place of George. The choice he makes at the end of the novella is an emotional one and we share in it. What would befall Lennie if George did not 'save' him?

Compare Lennie with Tiny Tim in *A Christmas Carol* and you see the writers' intent to draw different emotions from readers. Lennie is designed purely to elicit empathy and a certain sense of responsibility from the reader. Tiny Tim we feel empathy for, but we have some hope for him; he isn't completely doomed. We are happy to explore moral dilemmas but can refrain from discussing emotional dilemma. What both Lennie and Tiny Tim do is allow us to explore issues of disability and our emotional attachment to those who live with it.[3] The portent of Tiny Tim's death is terrible and shocking whereas Lennie's is a blessing and a salvation.

Of course, getting students to think as both a writer and a reader is key. We aren't helping students if we focus exclusively on one domain or the other. Today is a writing lesson. Tomorrow is a reading lesson. Writers are readers and we intend to make students both. We just need to help them connect the two disciplines. That's why I get students to construct their own characters when reading a novel so that they learn how a writer develops a character and practise that skill themselves, particularly with regard to the emotional impact of their choices. I give them a list and ask them to pick three options:

- Describe the sound of their footsteps.

- Describe their shoes.

- Describe the way the character walks/sits/writes/opens a door.

- Describe the smell of the character. Describe their perfume/aftershave/deodorant.

- Describe their voice. Focus on what makes their voice different to others'.

- Describe their reputation.

- Describe an action. It must be something kind, cruel or odd that they do.

- Describe their hands as they do something.

- Describe their silhouette.

- Describe how other characters feel about them.

---

3   This is an issue that is close to my heart as one of my daughters has cerebral palsy.

- Describe how the character treats people.
- Describe the character's relationship with their family.
- Describe the character through their relationship with others.
- Describe the temperature of the character and how that links to them as a person.
- Describe what makes the character sad or happy.
- Describe how other characters treat this person.
- Describe their hair. Be specific about colour, texture and the way it has been cut.
- Describe the clothes the character is wearing, but focus on the fabrics or where the items were bought.
- Describe the colour they are wearing and why they wear that particular colour.
- Describe the accessories they wear.
- Describe how their clothes link to their hair in some way.
- Describe how the character is an ugly version of someone famous.
- Describe their personality.
- Describe how the character looks at an object or a person.
- Describe their eyes. Include the colour, the size of the pupils and the way in which they move.
- Give the character's name and then explain how it suits them.
- Describe what they are not like. *He was not tall, not thin and not clever.*
- Describe what this person used to be like. *They used to be fun, keen and friendly.*
- Describe the character's reaction to something.
- Describe the one thing that makes this character contrast with all the others in the setting.
- Use a line of dialogue to show the character's personality.
- Describe how the character contrasts with the setting they are in.

- Describe the character's attempts to hide in the setting.

So, I could have a student who chooses the following three aspects:

- Describe their perfume/aftershave/deodorant.
- Describe their hands as they do something.
- Describe their silhouette.

Then I get them to attach an emotion to these, trying to avoid anger and happiness. Not all characters are heroes or villains; we can have moral ambiguity. I might get them to create a secretive, paranoid, optimistic or jealous character. How would you make a character secretive? You could use the perfume as a hint. Something you wouldn't notice at first. The hands could be so white as to be almost translucent. Their silhouette could be indefinable; their shadow blends too easily with other shadows.

By getting students to explore their own choices, they are more aware of the choices a writer makes. Identifying options helps students to see them in a text. All too often, we are expecting students to make big leaps with analysis. This approach helps to scaffold both the reading and the writing. I simply ask students which of these techniques Dickens uses in his description of Scrooge in *A Christmas Carol*. The beauty of this is that students create their own when they realise that the list doesn't fit the text. An explicit list helps to scaffold reading and writing. Plus, it mimics what an expert reader does. Students will build a stored memory of different approaches to describing a character so, when faced with a new one, they have a resource to use.

More lists

A PowerPoint of abstract nouns, especially emotions, is incredibly useful. The emotions can be different or variations of the same feeling (angry, frustrated, annoyed, seething, livid). Students can be great mimickers (you should see their impression of me), but they need a starting point. The teacher is one source, but they need others. Plus, teachers are not walking, talking thesauruses. Well, not all of us.

The process is quite simple. After we read a text and we are analysing it, I put up a list of abstract nouns and get students, in pairs, to discuss which words they'd associate with the section or with a particular character. I tend not to display the list when reading the text to avoid overloading students. I use it mainly for summarising and synthesising ideas.

- What are we supposed to feel towards this character?

- What is the writer trying to teach us?

- Summarise what the text says about X.

They search for abstract nouns in the text. Idea forming is a hard process to verbalise and we occasionally need to provide students with the tools to articulate abstract thoughts. When we read we don't normally name our feelings, so we are asking students to do something that isn't automatic. We have to teach them to articulate the experience, so they need guidance. Plus, the ideas encountered are often unfamiliar and so students don't have preformed conceptions. I should imagine I would struggle to articulate what the experience of bungee jumping is like if I'd only read about it once. It takes time and consideration and this isn't always an available luxury. If only we could say, we'll read this chapter today but I will ask you for your feelings on it next week, so you have time to think and formulate ideas. But, instead we ask, 'What do you feel?' 'Confused. OK, can anybody think of some better words we can use instead of confused?' And so it goes on.

A list of words can help to scaffold the formation and articulation of an idea. Students might have something in their head, but they need the language to express it.

5. ONE SENTENCE

Less able students tend to struggle when analysing whole texts; they mention several parts at once and so in superficial detail. In truth, the quantity of information swamps their thinking.

The new GCSE English exams have a connected strand. They rely on students being able to comment on language choices, comment on the effect and discuss the writer's intent. There is no getting away from this. We need students to become experts. I've developed a starter to use with less able students. Students come in, write down a sentence or two from the last lesson's reading and start analysing it. They do this most lessons and, as a result, their confidence has grown and so too have their skills of analysis. The process goes: words, purpose, feelings, techniques.

The Phantom slowly, gravely, silently approached. When it came, Scrooge bent down upon his knee; for in the very air through which this Spirit moved it seemed to scatter gloom and mystery.[4]

1   First, students spot and circle the key words. What words are the most important here?

    Gravely, silently, Phantom, gloom and mystery.

This starts students off with something simple. There's no right or wrong. During this stage, I reinforce each selected word using the correct grammatical term.

    Student: I spotted gravely and silently.

    Me: Yes, you have spotted two adverbs.

The hope is that they will make the leap and offer word classes themselves. I am modelling confidence with the terminology. Of course, they will make mistakes and it is important to talk about why and how. A fear of getting it wrong makes students either brazen or hesitant. My advice is to embody the idea that grammar can be tricky and requires thought before we give an answer. Most teachers, and I include myself, need to think before they give an answer about grammar because it is often dependent on context and minor

---

4   Dickens, *A Christmas Carol*, p. 76.

detail. As in mathematics, it needs some working out. I avoid getting students to answer straightaway. Time to think is necessary.

I also help students with the mistake when they give an incorrect answer. The instinct is to automatically correct the student but this propels the idea that there is a quick answer. When my daughters were learning to speak, we often repeated the correct word when they made a mistake.

Daughter: I runned to the end.

Me: ... ran ...

Daughter: I ran to the end.

Over time, she made the mistake less often. However, there was no negativity in the process; it allowed her to self-correct. Ideally, we want students to self-correct and we can help them do that.

Student: I think it's an adjective.

Teacher: What's our rule for spotting an adjective?

Student: An adjective describes a noun.

Teacher: So is it describing a noun?

Student: No.

Teacher: What other rules have we got for spotting the word class?

Note that I use 'our' when describing the rules. We have a shared understanding and collective approach. What's our rule for identifying verbs? It is incredibly helpful to have these rules clear in our heads. Grammar outlines the rules behind the language and we need to be clear about them. Getting it wrong just gives us another opportunity to revisit the rules. We often cast sneers towards 'the grammar police' without thinking about what directs them: the law. And we should have clear rules for identifying aspects of grammar. What's your rule for identifying a verb? Noun? Pronoun? Adjective? Adverb? Always start with the rule. This avoids the 'erm ... erm ... it's ... a verb' guessing game.

2 Then, we look at the purpose of the sentence. To frame this for students, I generally put up the following phrases:

To show us

To teach us

In the past, I've focused on feelings or techniques when getting students to analyse texts, but recently I have felt that purpose should be at the forefront. Get the purpose and the understanding follows. All too often, I have left the discussion about purpose until the end. We have spotted word classes, techniques and feelings and then, last of all, talked about why the writer chose specific versions of these things. This way, I am starting with the purpose. Starting with feelings can be problematic as sometimes we can't always articulate what it is we are feeling. Emotions are messy and can be hard to explain.

What is the writer trying to do here?

To show us the power and influence of the ghost. To show us how Scrooge is affected by the ghost. To teach us that the future is scary.

3 The next step is to start on the feelings. What are the different feelings we experience in this sentence?

Feel sorry for Scrooge. Feel scared of the ghost. Feel impressed with the ghost's power.

At each of these stages, we are referring back to the language in the quotation. What words make you feel sorry? What words show us that the future is scary? We develop meaning without using the shortcut methods of technique spotting and regurgitating clichés. We explore meaning and build it up in layers.

4   The final step explores techniques.

To get to this point, we have talked about words, purpose and effect, which inverts the analytical approach students usually use: I spot a technique; I explain the effect of the technique; I explain why the writer chose that technique.

A list. A pair. A short sentence.

At this point, students have a wealth of understanding to connect these elements together.

Dickens uses a list of adverbs to reflect the slow pace at which the ghost moves and the triplet also hints at its movement being rhythmic, as if the ghost moves like the ticking of a clock, moving towards the end.

Dickens' use of a short sentence here is uncommon. Usually, he describes the ghosts in great detail, yet here the ghost is described briefly, reflecting the fear and shock caused by this figure. It is somehow too scary to describe in any detail.

Dickens uses a pair of abstract nouns, 'gloom' and 'mystery', to create the atmosphere that follows the ghost. It suggests that there is a greater 'mystery' causing the 'gloom'.

I am incredibly interested in looking at structure and at internal structures that help aid meaning. This has been quite successful, and students have embraced it. But, most importantly, the consistency of the approach has worked well with lower attaining students. Eventually, it changes their internal thought processes so they think about the purpose and effect sooner, rather than as an afterthought to half a page of mindless rambling.

In the exams, students will be able to analyse a sentence in detail, linking it to other parts of the text and, therefore, show knowledge of the whole text. Without this approach, they will try to write about all the techniques and ideas at the same time. We need to channel their thinking. It's quite a simple approach, and it leads to a crap acronym – WPFT (words/purpose/feelings/techniques) – but it does help students to develop their thinking and is how I want them to think in the exam.

6. KNOWLEDGE OF THE TEXT

It can be surprising how much knowledge students have about storytelling. They regularly consume stories on TV and in film, yet they tend not to draw on that knowledge in the classroom. The job of the teacher here is, again, to show them the relevance of the knowledge they have of storytelling conventions. How the Marvel film *Thor* starts is relevant. How the makers of a science fiction programme introduce each new baddie is relevant. How *EastEnders* keeps several plots running at once is relevant. Our students have experienced thousands of openings, endings, developments, deaths and characters, and it is our job to draw on that. I tend to start with questions like:

- Why don't we have three characters called Bob who each have blonde hair and glasses in one story?

- Why don't villains wear T-shirts emblazoned with the phrase 'I am the story's bad guy so now watch me do bad stuff'?

- Two characters have spent years getting together. Now they're getting married and it is perfect. What happens next?

These are narrative conventions that every student knows. They know that we don't have three Bobs because it would be confusing for the reader. They know that villains are not identified from the beginning to make the story more surprising and unpredictable. They know that just when things seem perfect, something will go wrong. It is important to use this knowledge.

At my school, we teach a unit on Victorian villains and a key part of that relates to their own knowledge of such characters. We have compared Mr Squeers from

Nicholas Nickleby to the Penguin from *Batman*: both are given physical attributes to imply their evil nature. The more students are aware of and able to discuss techniques for characterisation and plot, the better they will be able to recognise them in texts and use them in their own writing.

Interesting questions to ask of students are:

- What is your experience of this genre or type of story?
- What is your knowledge of this type of storytelling?
- What is your knowledge of characters?
- What is your knowledge of settings?

The knowledge of how stories work is hidden somewhere in the student's brain. We don't really need to teach it, we just need to bring it to the forefront. This story starts with no description of the setting. Is that common? Why do you think the writer has done that? We need to take students' knowledge, secure it and improve it.

7. VOCABULARY

Sir, I would say that Piggy is a masochistic character who, in a way, contrasts with the sadistic Jack.

This one comment signalled a massive shift in understanding for a student in my class. Without the words 'masochistic' and 'sadistic', they would probably have said something along the lines of:

Sir, I would say that Piggy is a weak character who, in a way, contrasts with the cruel Jack.

One comment shows an insightful understanding of the characters and the other a superficial one. I'd like to say it took hours of teaching; it didn't. The table that follows helped the individual make the comment. The student then gave me examples of how Piggy provided opportunities for people to be cruel to him and how Jack let slip his enjoyment at being cruel to others.

Example vocabulary sheet

Barbarity: being brutal or inhuman.	Ferocity: violently cruel or like a wild beast, person or aspect.	Malice: a desire to inflict injury, harm or suffering on another because of meanness or an impulse.	Viciousness: deliberate cruelty.	Sadism: to take enjoyment from inflicting pain on others.
Ruthlessness: acting without pity or compassion.	Masochism: to take enjoyment from having pain inflicted on you.	Callousness: a hardened or unsympathetic attitude.	Depravity: to commit morally bad or evil actions.	Brutality: the quality of being cruel, savage, inhuman.
Inhumanity: not human or lacking human feelings such as sympathy, warmth or compassion.	Mercilessness: showing no mercy or compassion.	Bloodthirsty: eager to shed blood.	Homicidal: wanting to kill people.	Spite: to desire to harm, annoy, frustrate or humiliate another person.
Crude: natural, blunt or underdeveloped.	Feral: having the characteristics of a wild animal.	Civilised: to be educated, refined and enlightened.	Uncivilised: to be uneducated or uncultured.	Being ill-bred: showing a lack of social breeding; being unmannerly or rude.

Source: Definitions adapted from www.dictionary.com

The format for using a vocabulary sheet is quite simple:

1 Give students the sheet.

2 Students draw the definitions of all twenty words in a simple, Pictionary-style sketch.

3 The whole class play a game of Pictionary.

4 The class play a game of Blockbusters to recall the definitions. What C is an adjective to describe something natural, blunt or underdeveloped?

5 Students learn the words for homework.

6 In the next lesson, students complete a multiple-choice test on the definitions.

7 In the following lesson, students complete a further test on definitions. What F is having the characteristics of a wild animal?

8 In a further lesson, students write a paragraph using as many of the words as possible.

I might vary the format, but in any case there is a lot of repetition and I am asking students for definitions. I keep going back to the new words. Who is the most feral character in *Lord of the Flies*? Remind me again, what does feral mean?

What I like about this is that I have now developed a kind of sociolect: a way of speaking that the class and I share. When I speak with another teacher we use what must seem to the students the equivalent of Parseltongue. This approach ensures we have a common language. At the core is repetition using different contexts. Drawing helps students to visualise the idea and convert it from the concrete to the abstract. The definitions allow students to attach the word to the meaning and identify how each word differs. Discussion helps students to secure the pronunciation of the word and see how they can fit it into a sentence. Writing helps students to secure how to use the words for meaning in their own work.

In the past, I'd say that my vocabulary as a teacher has concentrated chiefly on clarity. I might have punctuated my speech with high-level vocabulary, but for the most part my language was Standard English and was neither that varied nor that complex. I was too concerned with having everyone understand me. Having used this bank of twenty words, I can get to complex and challenging ideas with a class far quicker than before.

Imagine giving directions to the city centre, but you can only use the words 'right' and 'left'. It would take a long time and be very vague; there's a strong chance that the person would not get there. Add words like 'roundabout', 'junction' and 'traffic lights' and they'll stand a better chance. Add specific street names and you add precision. We often use limited direction in the classroom, like 'left' or 'right', when actually we need precise names and prepositions such as 'onto Bridge Street'. When I think of how vocabulary is taught, I worry. Look at how we use phrases like 'word of the week' and 'wow words'. We concentrate on the individual meanings of words or on a bank of randomly selected vocabulary. We rarely look at the context and rarely do we spend enough time looking at the vocabulary and register associated with certain topics. We make endless lists of words. Lists for analysis. Lists for talking about poems. Lists for talking about photosynthesis. Maybe we need to look at the language we naturally use and how to get students to translate this into academic Parseltongue. We only have to look at modern foreign language departments to see this in place.

Of course, words are only part of it; there's grammar and syntax too. How often do we look at the language in a lesson to check whether it is focused on clarity and on all students making progress? Perhaps we are being counterproductive. Starting with the basics isn't always the best principle. To learn a language, you need to immerse yourself. Surely we should be exposing students to rich worlds of vocabulary rather than a trickling brook of the odd word here and there. Complex, precise vocabulary should be used all the time and that starts and ends with the teacher. We should be working harder to get students to speak our language, but first we must identify it. We must be adding to the class vocabulary daily, weekly and monthly. Our common tongue is standard, generic and imprecise for the job we need it to do. It is helpful at times, but it will not lift up students' souls with the beauty of words nor raise their academic success through understanding.

So what does this look like in the classroom? In mine, it is usually done through vocabulary lists and constantly exploring new words or revising familiar ones. Every lesson and every task is an opportunity to look at words: I praise students when they use a new word in their writing and I use explanation to further their vocabulary. If students don't have the words, then they can't explain the idea fully, accurately or appropriately.

In a typical week, all my classes will be engaging with words. This has looked like the following:

Year 7 – Collected synonyms for the word 'vulnerable' linked to the opening of *Jane Eyre*.

Year 8 – Explored the precise meaning of words in *Macbeth*.

Year 9 – Explored the different meanings of the word 'exposure', linked to the poem of the same name by Wilfred Owen.

Year 10 – Revised ten words associated with villains.

Year 11 – Researched words they are unfamiliar with in *Romeo and Juliet* for homework.

On top of that, I will routinely do the following:

• Select students to offer definitions of words. Ready recall of definitions is something students need to get better at; we need it to become a common occurrence rather than an occasional surprise when they find a word they don't know.

• Ask students to select words they don't understand in a text and look them up in a dictionary.

• Give students lists of words when writing or exploring a text so that they can articulate ideas clearly.

• Collect words from students to create new lists. This one is a great homework. Find four words to describe Macbeth's personality. Collate them together and students have a great starting point for an essay.

• Use literary vocabulary tests to reinforce the terminology needed to discuss texts.

• Test students on definitions. Give them ten words (all taken from a GCSE text) and ask them to select the correct definition from a list of options.

- Use weekly spelling tests to reinforce vocabulary.

- Use a new words board. Every time a new word is introduced in class, a student writes it on the board.

As a department, we look at past papers and select words which might be unfamiliar to students. Plus, there is the reading of texts. I am a big believer in giving students complex texts and discovering what they do and don't know. For more ideas on how to develop vocabulary use, I'd highly recommend Alex Quigley's *Closing the Vocabulary Gap*.[5]

---

5   A. Quigley, *Closing the Vocabulary Gap* (Abingdon: Routledge, 2018).

Chapter 4
HOW TO TEACH ESSAY WRITING

Sometimes, secondary schools assume that students will arrive in Year 7 with the ability to write a complete essay. Sadly this isn't the case, and it isn't the fault of primary teachers; it is just the way the education system works. From a writing perspective, primary schooling focuses on fluency and a set number of styles. The secondary curriculum does all that and adds essay writing into the mix.

Essay writing is problematic because we make a lot of assumptions about who has taught students this skill. I don't think I was ever explicitly taught how to write an essay; instead, I learned through trial and error and, if I am honest, more the latter than the former. How many secondary curriculums feature the explicit teaching of essay writing? Not that many, I'd wager. In fact, I'd place a fairly substantial bet that very few have a unit or even a series of lessons dedicated to it because of the amount of content that needs to be covered.

The essay is simplified or refined thought. It is the sieve of learning in the classroom. It shows how a student has interpreted or used the knowledge taught and how they have formed new ideas along the way. A good essay is a thing of beauty. A bad one is painful (to read and to write) and time consuming. An essay shows how we think. It shows the level of our thinking. That's why essay writing needs to have a stronger place in the curriculum, even in primary schools. The drawback is that, compared to other forms – story writing, newspaper writing – essay writing isn't very sexy.

Essays are the staple of writing in secondary schools and we are fools if we do not acknowledge this. They show the synthesis of ideas. They show condensed thinking. They show a hypothesis. A test shows a student's knowledge and understanding, yet an essay shows how they think. What we get, however, are piecemeal essays. Look at any exam paper and you see the components of an essay. The questions call for an essay dissected into constituent parts. The twelve-mark question is simply a paragraph. We have dissected the essay so much in some subjects that all that's left is body parts in a jar. We are assessing students on their ability to play 'Chopsticks' when they could be aspiring to Mozart.

The latest GCSE English literature exam has students writing the equivalent of three essays in two hours and fifteen minutes. These are long, extended pieces of discourse. The preparation that teachers have taken students through has not always been as helpful as it might be. Essays can be taught as dot-to-dot writing. Repeat everything the teacher has told you, and here are some silly structural devices to include. In that case, you end up with the student as a metaphorical photocopier of ideas. Their success is dependent on copying the teacher's fixed model and their mark dependent on how close they are. That's why essay plans are so dangerous. They promote a fixed model of writing.

An essay teaches us a lot about a student. It teaches us about their understanding of plot, character, language, themes and structure. It teaches us about their ability to concentrate at length on an idea. It teaches us about how much they have listened. It teaches us about how well or how poorly they have followed instructions.

1. 10%, 50%, 20%, 20%

It is pretty hard for students to see what it is that needs to be developed when trying to improve their essay skills. They are raised to write and tell stories from an early age, but knowing what a good essay should or shouldn't look like is something they haven't encountered. We have stories in our blood, yet essays are alien. Students are in the eye of the storm when writing; it is always hard to see the impact when you are at the centre.

This approach is a nice and easy one that helps students to see what they have got to do. I start by getting them to draft their essays. Then I show them this:

Description 90%

Explanation 10%

Linking 0%

Opinion 0%

Typically, this is how students write a first draft. The emphasis is on cramming everything in, so they list or describe things. It is usually drivel. I then show students the next step up:

Description 35%

Explanation 35%

Linking 15%

Opinion 15%

I simply ask students: what is the difference between the two? They start to see how the other aspects are important and relate it to their own work. I get them to assign the figures to their own work. If necessary, they can highlight the different aspects – students love to highlight things.

Finally, I show them this:

Description 10%

Explanation 50%

Linking 20%

Opinion 20%

The great thing about this is that it helps students to quickly understand the purpose of their writing. Progress becomes about reducing the descriptive and increasing the explanatory (the more able students focus on links and opinions). The relationship between the numbers is important. Writing isn't about chucking everything in the pot and hoping it works. There is an ingredients list, and it does matter how much of each thing you put in a recipe. We have all mixed up a tablespoon and teaspoon. Have a go yourself with this sample paragraph. What percentages do you think the student is using?

Dickens presents Scrooge as a character that starts off mean but becomes warm and softens as the events in the story happen. We see him at the start being cruel and direct to characters, but after each ghost we see him becoming kinder and friendlier in the story. In the opening, we see that even the 'dogs' of the blind men are scared of him. Dickens uses 'flint' to highlight how cruel and sharp the character is. At the end we see him openly embracing and being kind to people. Scrooge becomes a kinder and friendlier person as a result of the ghost. [1]

Hopefully, you'll see that the student is focused on describing things, but there is very little explanation here. It is as if the student needs to be constantly asked why as they are writing. All too often, writing is about content rather than purpose. This approach addresses that. Most teachers are familiar with the PEE model and its various chimera-like children. Students are taught to make a point (P) and then provide evidence (E) for that point. Finally, they finish their paragraph with some explanation (the final E). The PEE form of analytical essay has its roots in content rather than skills. Students are taught parrot-like, and quite dully, to use this structure. They are not thinking about the skills they are showing, but fitting into an image of what an essay must look like. By placing the emphasis on skills rather than content, however, you change how students write an essay. Helping them to see that they are describing more than they are explaining is more helpful than just telling a student that they need more explanation in their essay and that they have only done a PE paragraph and not a PEE paragraph. After looking at the percentages with students, I will then spend time looking at explanation and at how they can use words, sentences and phrases to help them explain things better.

This approach can work for other things too. Recently, when analysing and writing speeches, I applied the percentages to the use of ethos, pathos and logos. Students

---

1   Dickens, *A Christmas Carol*, p. 12.

were able to explore how various writers played around with the balance for effect. At the same time, we explored how the context might change the percentages and this caused quite a bit of discussion. What's more important when announcing a war, pathos or ethos?

We might offer this as a starting point and then see if there is a need to change the ratio between the elements based on context:

30% ethos

20% pathos

50% logos

For a funeral speech, a student might need to increase the pathos. For a head teacher's speech, a student might want to increase the ethos. For a politician's, a student might want to reduce logos completely. The relationship between the three elements is key and leads to a very useful analysis of speech.

2. METAPHORS – FIGURATIVE LANGUAGE

We want students to achieve clarity while discussing complex concepts and synthesising ideas of their own. For years, teachers have used the strategy of showing pictures and asking students to relate them to a text. Images help to elicit complex interpretations. What we haven't done as much is get students to use those images to inform explanation in their essays.

Take the following sentence I've used with a class for *An Inspector Calls*:

The inspector attacks the foundations of the Birling family.

Metaphors are a way to extend and develop students' interpretations, and provide a shortcut to abstract thinking. Too often, vocabulary can lead us into a dictionary corner: a student has learned *broadly* what the word 'socialism' means, but do they understand its relevance to the play and the society in which it is based? Here, metaphorical 'foundations' take on a role. The inspector isn't just attacking the people but the ideas they live by, their society, their origins, their education and their way of life. He is attacking their very basis: the thing that is holding them up as a family and in society. Attack a foundation and everything falls. One little metaphor can say so much, so it is a flagrant waste not to use them: they are the diamonds of interpretation.

Let's take the original metaphor and rework it. What happens if we explore the choice of verbs?

The inspector destroys the foundations of the Birling family.

The inspector attacks the foundations of the Birling family.

The inspector picks away at the foundations of the Birling family.

The inspector blows up the foundations of the Birling family.

'Destroys' and 'blows up' suggest malice and an evil intent which would be contradictory to Priestley's purpose. 'Picks away' suggests things are slow and slight. 'Attacks' is certainly aggressive but suggests an ongoing process that hasn't yet achieved destruction. A better word could be 'challenges', but 'attacks' might be the verb we decide upon because Priestley wants to undermine the foundations of the Birlings so that they are level with the Smiths or the Joneses.

Once you have explored the use of one metaphor, it is easier to introduce more:

Eric is a ticking time bomb.

The inspector is a cat among the pigeons.

Sheila is a lighthouse in a storm.

114

Sheila is the crack in the wall.

We can have fun getting students to explore each metaphor in detail. Here's an example:

Sheila is the crack in the wall because she sees the potential of treating people fairly: she sees what is potentially on the other side. The rest of the characters are fixed and immovable by comparison. A crack getting bigger over time will cause a wall to fall down, and Sheila might be considered the start of this process. The events of the play show the crack forming and possibly later, after the conclusion, they will expand.

The great thing about the use of metaphor is that you have to develop and extend it in the explanation. A student will have to talk about the crack, the bricks, the other side of the wall and the process of change. In fact, the metaphor crosses the whole play and relates to the structure. At the start, Sheila is part of the wall: a person who accepts and maintains the idea of social inequality. As the play progresses she starts to see the error of her ways and challenges the rules governing society. She represents a crack which is not quite big enough to break the wall but, in time … Add a few quotations, and we are near a reasoned and developed interpretation.[2]

The great thing about using metaphor in non-fiction is that you automatically feel the need to explain the metaphor after using it. Too often I've seen students with great ideas, but their lack of descriptive prowess hinders the development. A metaphor necessarily creates an interpretation and begs explanation.

You can use personification and simile to develop the writing further. Honesty sleeps in *Macbeth*. Of course, students must use them sparingly and carefully and this is what I tell them, but it makes for some great interpretations — and some crazy ones too. Apparently, Macbeth is like a window cleaner because he is always trying to see

---

2   Some possible metaphors to use: smashing through the glass ceiling, a bomb waiting to explode, a mirror, a painting, a lighthouse, a steam train, a wrecking ball, a torch, a magnifying glass and a microscope.

through the muddle and confusion of things. (Oh, and avoid metaphors relating to popular culture. Describing the events of *An Inspector Calls* as being like the TV show *Big Brother* is unlikely to work.)

3. WRITING AN ESSAY TOGETHER

Modelling writing a paragraph on the board can be very powerful. It shows students what a good example looks like and, while writing, you can commentate, thereby uncovering the choices and decisions a writer makes. A few years ago a colleague revealed that this was the approach he used with lower sets and, to this day, it is something I regularly do with classes of all abilities. Plus it keeps them quiet and focused for an hour.

With more challenging classes, I might develop the process slowly. Better to ease them in gently with a paragraph or so and then build up to longer pieces over time. Another way I use it is as a solution to a problem. Say you have given the students a writing task that they are generally struggling with. I might use this approach to rescue them. Are you finding this difficult? I tell you what, why don't we do this together? Another way of getting them engaged is to turn it into a competition and, like the *Star Wars* opening, make the text disappear. Students have to be quick to keep up and you create a sense of urgency.

So, what does the process look like? Simple. Open a word document. Have it displayed on the interactive whiteboard. Type an essay. The students copy it down. Then they go back through the text and highlight key choices or decisions. I'll often spend a whole lesson writing an essay in this way. Then, in the next lesson, students attempt one on their own. Get them familiar with the process then repeat it until it becomes automatic. The first essay-writing lesson is a collective one. It is a two way process: I will constantly ask questions, such as:

Look! All my sentences start with 'the'. Anybody got any ideas about how I can fix this?

What do you think my next point should be?

Have I covered this idea enough?

I've used the writer's name too many times. What can I do?

Is this quotation effective? Could I pick a better one?

I model the process and not just the result. Modelling isn't about waving a good example around and asking students to copy it but in their own words. It is about teaching them what good writers do during the process of composition. Over time, students will have a collection of good examples in their books and a range of writing experiences. They are simply working on their 'muscle memory' and how it feels to be reflecting on your work.

4. MICRO TEACHING

Demands on time and the pressure to get through the curriculum often have a negative impact: we end up trying to do everything at once. In this chapter, I've mentioned three different approaches to essay writing in the classroom and they all work in isolation, but what happens towards the end of term or year is that all three aspects are tried in quick succession. Teachers will try to teach the semicolon, use parody, show examples while drafting and learn seven quotations from the Bible simultaneously. We chuck everything at the students. I take the opposite path: the more pressurised things become, the more I focus on the content. Effective teaching isn't about overloading. It is about clarity and decluttering. I tend to focus on narrow aspects, unpicking a thread and spending a lesson making students better at that one small thing. Little changes can have a big impact.

Here's one such thread: use 'but' or 'yet' when explaining complex ideas.

The poem conveys how the experience is painful <u>yet</u> important to the mother.

I'd spend a whole lesson looking at this and developing ideas. It might involve exploring what other words I could use instead of 'but' or 'yet'. It might look at the relationship of the two ideas in the poem: how some experiences hurt and how we learn lessons from them. It might look at the rest of the poem and produce more example sentences. It might take that sentence and build the rest of the paragraph. Whichever way we look at it, I make sure the students know that specific structure and will use it on pain of death in their writing.

Here's a list of some other minor tweaks I have used in lessons and as exam hacks:

1   Develop your interpretations by building up meaning – suggests/shows/ symbolises.

The poem shows us a mother reflecting on a child going to war, which suggests how much this has had an impact on her. The poem symbolises the struggle families have in war.

---

2   Use adverbs at the start of sentences – Literally ... Figuratively ... Symbolically ...

Literally, the poem is about a mother's loss. Figuratively, the poem explores how a mother's bond with a child is constant. Symbolically, the poem is about how soldiers' lives are ignored and taken for granted. [3]

---

3   More adverbs – physically, mentally, emotionally, spiritually, psychologically. Use these adverbs to help explain ideas in poems.

'Exposure' explores how war affects people physically and mentally, but 'Poppies' focuses on how it affects people spiritually and psychologically.

---

3   C. Spalding, Teaching ideas: what has worked for me recently?, *Teacher's Notes* [blog] (1 May 2017). Available at: http://mrscspalding.blogspot.com/2017/05/teaching-ideas-what-has-worked-for-me.html.

4   Lists are your friends – list <u>emotions/techniques/ideas/phrases</u>.

The poet <u>challenges, explores and develops</u> his <u>fear, anger and frustration</u> of war with <u>lists and rhetorical questions</u>.

5   Think about the verbs you use to describe what the poet is doing – <u>challenges/reflects/embodies/attacks</u>. The verb you use helps you to explain how the poet is presenting their message.

The poet <u>attacks</u> the leaders of war – the voice is aggressive and angry.

The poet <u>reflects</u> the loss a parent faces in war – the voice is calm.

6   Use adverbs to evaluate the poem – <u>stereotypically/unusually/typically/realistically/unconventionally/surprisingly/convincingly/unconvincingly</u>.

Owen <u>realistically</u> conveys the war from the perspective of the soldiers on the battlefield and challenges how other poets present war <u>stereotypically</u> and <u>unrealistically</u>.

7   Combine techniques together – use '<u>and</u>' and link words/techniques.

The poet uses lists <u>and</u> exaggeration <u>to highlight</u> how bad things were.

The poet uses the adjectives 'small' <u>and</u> 'tiny' <u>to make</u> the reader feel superior.

8   Put an adjective before a technical term.

The writer uses <u>violent</u> verbs and <u>physical</u> adjectives to …

9 Think about using one of these words to sum up the structure of the poem – a journey/a discovery/a realisation – then add some adverbs/adjectives.

The poem is a psychological journey from despair to hope.

The poem is an emotional realisation.

10 Use the phrase 'it could also' and add a further interpretation.

It could also be a study of the complexity of war.

11 Use tentative statements – perhaps/maybe/possibly.

Perhaps the writer intends the reader to …

12 Use lots of one-word quotations.

The writer uses the words 'pain' and 'torture' to highlight the endless suffering experienced by the men.

13 Show off with your emotions – avoid using simple emotions like happiness, sadness, anger. Use emotions like frustration, envy, dismay.

The poem explores the boredom, apathy and emptiness of war on the front line.

When completed with a class, I print them off as a crib sheet. The little things add together over time to make the whole better.

5. COMPARISON OF TEXTS

I am pretty short for a man. Think of Curley in *Of Mice and Men* but with less curls, less aggression and fewer gloves. I know I am pretty short for a man because lots of people, especially men, generally look down on me (and I don't mean figuratively). My understanding of shortness comes from the relationship between my own height and other points of reference. Now, I am not hung up about my height,[4] but I use it as an example to show how one's understanding is linked to external reference points. That's why we should constantly be getting students to look at their own work and see the relationship with other pieces. I do feel, however, that peer assessment doesn't help with this.

Peer assessment often seems to involve a student conjuring up a judgement from nowhere. They usually have insufficient experience to form any decent analytical idea as to whether the work is good or not. All too often they opt for glib comments on how the spelling needs improving or how they like the way the student has used punctuation. When students compare their work with another's, then you get more fruitful pieces of assessment. I have read millions of pieces of writing, so when I look at one I have clear ideas about what a typical student should be producing. My assessment and judgement has a basis. Students don't have that knowledge, but shoving two examples together helps them to see if X is better than Y. Then the peer discussion can be about why X is better than Y, but also what Y does better than X. The relationship between the pieces can be explored and fruitful comparisons can be made.

Putting comparative elements together in lessons is crucial for developing a picture in students' heads of how texts can differ. By comparing two texts, students can see different angles or approaches.

The following is an example using a single sentence, but I usually use a longer text with a class.

---

4   That's why I keep mentioning it.

Student example: *The writer makes Lady Macbeth a mean character to create tension.*

Teacher example: *Lady Macbeth is used by Shakespeare to show audiences the potential for ruthlessness that Macbeth has.*

When comparing the two examples, you might pick up on the following in the teacher piece:

- Change in subject – Lady Macbeth to the writer.

- Emphasis on the choice rather than the writer.

- Change in verb – 'used' rather than 'makes'.

- Uses 'Shakespeare' rather than 'the writer'.

- Makes reference to the audience.

- Longer answer.

The great thing about using examples as points of comparison is that it draws attention to what the student has done and makes them reflect on the writing process. I always start with the following sentence stems:

Mine's better because ...

The example is better than mine because ...

The key to this is the relationship with the text. That's why I am prone to writing at the same time as students and then showing my work on the board. Examples shown at the start of the process are good, but I think that they are even more important at the end. Students need to make mistakes and learn from them. Again, this is another way to promote dialogue about writing.

6. LEARN FROM THE GREATS

How many times have students read an academic essay in your classroom? The majority of students read quasi-academic essays. The teacher probably wrote one in their planning, preparation and assessment (PPA) time and based it on what the GCSE exam board expects a 9 will look like. That's why we have had point, evidence, explanation (PEE) reinforced and repeated again and again. It gives the impression of structured thought, but it doesn't replicate genuine academic essays. In truth, they don't use it, nor do I recall university lecturers telling me that I needed to PEE more in my essays. Find and print off superb essays. Read them in class. Take sentences from them. Use them. Talk about them. Return to them again and again.

I have used the following quotes from Mark Van Doren about *Macbeth*.

- 'Concerned wholly with sensation and catastrophe … terror rather than pity.'[5]
- 'It is furthermore a world in which nothing is certain to keep its shape.'[6]
- 'Shakespeare again has enclosed his evil within a universe of good, his storm centre within wide areas of peace.'[7]

The great thing about these lines, displayed around the classroom, is the level of understanding they elicit. We answered the following questions:

- What does it mean?

- Where do we see it in the play?

- Do we agree with the statement?

The level of discussion was raised. We spent a good lesson exploring the idea that *Macbeth* was about 'terror and not pity' and had a debate about whether we pity Macbeth and whether you can experience terror and pity at the same time. Aim high and pull students up with you!

---

5   M. Van Doren, *Macbeth*. In L. F. Dean (ed.), *Shakespeare: Modern Essays in Criticism* (Oxford: Oxford University Press, 1967), pp. 346–360 at p. 346.
6   Ibid, p. 348.
7   Ibid, p. 360.

Chapter 5
HOW TO TEACH NON-FICTION

Non-fiction is English teacher Marmite. There are many of us who turn off at the thought of it, thinking, 'I didn't spend years at university to analyse a newspaper. I studied the pioneers of modern literature, for goodness sake! The last thing I want to do is study the work of a two-bit hack.'

The problem with teaching non-fiction is how rapidly we reduce it according to generic features. This is a diary. These are the features of a diary. Here is an example of a diary. Spot the features of a diary. Now, write your own diary. This approach produces generic writing. I have read countless examples by students and, overall, the issue lies with the reductive process of teaching non-fiction and not with the individual. You'll have a great newspaper article if it has alliteration in the title! (Yeh, right.) Non-fiction has heart and we teach it as if it doesn't.

Admittedly, non-fiction doesn't lend itself to lessons as easily as poetry or fiction. But it is more accessible and probably read more often by students out of choice. As a teenager, I read libraries full of non-fiction on the making of TV shows and films. I loved them. I didn't read many novels, but I'd read *TV Zone* from cover to cover and learned *all* about the making of *Star Trek* and *Doctor Who*. Non-fiction is grounded in reality; it seeks to report the world as it is and that is undervalued. Fiction involves imagining, visualising and constructing a world in our heads while non-fiction involves trying to understand our own. I could tell you endless facts about *Doctor Who* and other TV shows. They are all relatively useless, but they helped me understand the shows and their production. I didn't want escapism when reading, I wanted knowledge and understanding. Of course, the two elements are interchangeable and fluid: students understand through experience and learn from knowledge.

Non-fiction should be a consistent reference point in the classroom. We should be switching constantly between it and fiction. Students shift levels of verbal formality all the time, yet 'code shifting' related to genre and text style rarely happens in the classroom. We section off lessons for poetry or non-fiction. Rarely do the two meet and mix. Non-fiction shouldn't be saved for a unit of work. Your lovely unit on persuasive texts may well be teaching students that non-fiction is boring.

The beauty of non-fiction is in its immediacy. Spending five weeks studying different examples of persuasive writing kills off interest, ideas and connection to the subject. Newspaper articles are written within minutes of the event. Diaries are written on the day. Letters are written as the writer thinks. Each of these texts are immediate. The writer didn't spend two months exploring how they might present their ideas and they didn't go through twenty drafts. They just got the ideas down on the page. You don't spend six weeks writing an email complaining about the description of an item you bought on the internet. While fiction needs attention, thought and time, non-fiction lives in the moment. It should be written in the moment. Read in the moment.

Pick non-fiction texts you personally find interesting. Don't obsess over making non-fiction fit the hole in the curriculum that needs filling. It can be separate. Keep a focus on immediacy; read quickly and write quickly. Show its relevance to now. Get students to think, react and discuss.

1. QUESTIONING

Questioning can work on so many levels with non-fiction. To properly understand the world, we need to ask the right questions. Usually, people cite open and closed questions as the main variants, but I think we can be more selective and intuitive with our questioning.

The older a child gets, sadly, the fewer questions they ask of us. My daughters couldn't stop asking questions in their toddler days, yet that dies down as kids enter their teenage years. We need to focus on getting our students to ask more and better questions. Here are some simple alternatives to standard questioning:

Questioning the alternatives: *Why not ...? Why doesn't ...? Why wouldn't ...?*

Questioning that aids evaluation: *Which is the best/least/most/weakest ...?*

Questioning that makes students take a position: *If you were against this, what would you say?*

Questioning the consequences: *If _____, then why _____?*

I like also to dress up the questioning and look at texts from different enquiring viewpoints. I take the classics and link the questioning to how detectives approach a crime. Sherlock Holmes would make inferences. Miss Marple would relate things to her own experience and knowledge. Poirot would look for the inconsistencies. Morse would look at the different perspectives.

I give students the following on cards or on a PowerPoint and we interrogate the text. They form questions of their own then pass them on to another group or pair. They are given sentence stems to help form their ideas. I love getting students to talk about non-fiction texts and this approach allows them to do it freely.

Sherlock Holmes – inferences/reading between the lines.

What clues are there that ...?

How do ____ and ____ link together?

What is the connection between _____ and _____?

I can infer from this that ...

This suggests that ...

It seems that ...

_____ evidence and _____ evidence show that ...

Miss Marple – relating to our own world/experience/knowledge.

Where have you seen this before?

What other subject has this? What skills from RE can you bring in to explain this?

This reminds me of ...

We saw this when ...

I notice that _____ has happened when _____ .

Poirot – looking for the flaws and inconsistencies.

Which bits don't add up?

Where have they contradicted themselves?

What are the weaknesses in their argument?

They say _____ , but it doesn't match up with _____ .

I notice that they say _____ , but later they say the opposite. I don't think they are completely certain because ...

Inspector Morse – looking at the perspectives.

What does the other person say?

How does this person's view differ from the rest? Does everybody agree with this point?

One person said _____ while the others said _____ .

From a different perspective, it can be seen that ...

I struggle with reducing or simplifying reading skills to a few key strategies as reading is a vast, complex and multilayered process, but this approach makes sure that there is a focus when interrogating a text. A while back, English teachers were led, by the infamous National Literacy Strategy, to believe that there were several strategies good readers employed.[1] For me, this was a simplification of the process of reading. For example, one strategy was to visualise a text. Yes, it made a nice activity, but it

---

1   See https://webarchive.nationalarchives.gov.uk/20100603153307/http://nationalstrategies. standards.dcsf.gov.uk/secondary/secondaryframeworks.

rarely engaged with the ideas in any depth. It was a simple consolidation task. Plus, if I only saw pictures when I read, I'd have a vastly oversimplified view of what was really going on. This approach, however, sets up students to interrogate the text.

Ideas are at the heart of English and, if we don't look at how students engage with them, we aren't really teaching. They might struggle with the answers, but every student can ask a question regardless of ability and they should be made to do so regularly. Questioning and ideas go hand in hand.

2. ISOLATE AND EXPLORE

The ability to spot good texts to use with students is developed through trial and error, but when you find a good text, you don't let it go. One of my favourites, because it is more relevant today than ever, is Jack London's *The People of the Abyss*. In the book, he explores (as an outsider) what it is like to live in poverty in the slums of Victorian London. The following extract explores the sad issue of child mortality:

I have talked with these children, here, there, and everywhere, and they struck me as being bright as other children, and in many ways even brighter. They have most active little imaginations. Their capacity for projecting themselves into the realm of romance and fantasy is remarkable. A joyous life is romping in their blood. They delight in music, and motion, and colour, and very often they betray a startling beauty of face and form under their filth and rags.

But there is a Pied Piper of London Town who steals them all away. They disappear. One never sees them again, or anything that suggests them. You may look for them in vain amongst the generation of grown-ups. Here you will find stunted forms, ugly faces, and blunt and stolid minds. Grace, beauty, imagination, all the resiliency of mind and muscle, are gone. [2]

2   J. London, *The People of the Abyss* (Project Gutenberg ebook edition, 2005 [Edinburgh: Thomas Nelson and Sons, 1903]), ch 23. Available at: http://www.gutenberg.org/files/1688/1688-h/1688-h.htm.

When presenting a text like this to students, I unpick one thread or idea first. Commonly, teachers will give students a list of questions designed to elicit understanding and engagement. I prefer something as simple as:

Give me three reasons why the writer uses the comparative 'brighter' to describe the children in the slums.

They give me the following reasons:

1   It highlights how they are the only good thing about this place.

2   There is a sense of optimism and hope that they could survive.

3   To suggest how the children are born innocent and happy, but the setting changes them.

4   To suggest how the children are similar to children in other parts of the country.

5   To create a sense of tragedy.

I remind them I only asked for three. Then I ask students to develop their interpretation further. How do you know that the children are the *only* good thing about the place?

You get students saying that the writer describes their 'blood' as joyous and then describes the rest of the people as 'stunted' and 'ugly'. It is at this point that you can clarify any misreadings or misunderstandings. It also forces students to make links across the text to justify an interpretation: all things that they will need to do at GCSE.

What this approach does is help you and the students to look at the text as a whole rather than as a catalogue of techniques. A comprehension task is OK, but it doesn't address the 'how' and the 'why' in enough detail for me. It ends up being a search and find activity. I like pulling the thread and seeing where it goes. Detailed understanding comes from detailed analysis, which, in turn, comes from obsessing over the nuances. Take the 'Pied Piper of London'. Pull and pull on that thread and see what you find:

- Pied Piper – removed rats and children – so connection between children and vermin.

- Pied Piper was a popular German legend.

- The parents never saw their children again as a result of his actions.

- Parents were responsible.

- Initially, the Pied Piper was seen as a saviour and do-gooder, but then as evil and villainous.

Comprehension tasks often focus on the techniques rather than the ideas. Put the ideas at the front and you can talk effectively about the choices the writer makes. If you start thinking solely about choices, then you struggle to explain the ideas behind them. We do need to change the dynamic in reading. Lead with ideas and not language choices.

3. SUMMARISING

Summarising has become relevant again and most exam boards address the skill within their specification in some manner. Often they refer to it as 'implied meaning' and the summary aspect is implied in the question. However, AQA are one example of an exam board with a specific summary question on the GCSE English language paper 2. For a long while, textual analysis formed the basis of pretty much all work in lessons, but now we need to teach students how to summarise a text. One of the reasons why they struggle with this is because of the phrase, 'write it in your own words'. When they receive this instruction, you get the text reduced rather than summarised. They copy out large chunks and pass it off as a summary.

I've already mentioned inference words in poetry – remember, these are often abstract nouns – but they can be used for all texts. If we take the extract from *The People of the Abyss*, we could attach the following inference words: 'ignorant', 'escapism', 'surprising', 'unexpected', 'pleasure'. This gets students used to attaching words to ideas rather than just repeating what happens in the text – this is the synthesis part of the summary.

Take this piece from the *Guardian*'s newspaper archive. It describes the events on the night the *Titanic* sunk:

> *Late last night the White Star officials in New York announced that a message had been received stating that the Titanic sank at 2.20 yesterday morning after all her passengers and crew had been transferred to another vessel. Later they admitted that many lives had been lost. An unofficial message from Cape Race, Newfoundland, stated that only 675 have been saved out of 2,200 to 2,400 persons on board. This was in some degree confirmed later by White Star officials in Liverpool, who said they were afraid the report was likely to prove true. Assuming that only 675 of the passengers and crew have been saved, and taking the smallest estimate of the number of people on board, the disaster is one of the most awful in the history of navigation, for at least 1,500 lives have been lost.[3]*

Compare the extract to this summary:

There was lots of confusion at the start and uncertainty about how many people survived and died as a result of the event. It was later discovered that, in reality, things had been far worse than expected.

Now we can ask some interesting questions:

• What words are summarising the text?

• Where can we find examples of these points in the original text?

• Can we rephrase things?

• What is missing?

---

3   *The Guardian*, The Titanic is sunk, with great loss of life (16 April 1912). Available at: https://www.theguardian.com/news/1912/apr/16/leadersandreply.mainsection.

'Summarise the text' seems such an easy and, probably, glib instruction to give to students, but it is a process that we don't look at often enough in lessons. I'll be bold and say that more time spent on summarising could improve students' thinking and writing overall. Precision in thinking has always separated the top from the rest in English. Clear and precise thoughts get the marks over rambling, vague and confused 'brain dribblings'. By getting students to look at their summary and its relationship with the text, you expose their understanding. You see what they have neglected, misunderstood or made up. Again, vocabulary is a key part of this. A student can find a billion clever examples of similes, but unless they have a coherent viewpoint about why they are used it remains technique vomiting. In the beginning was the word. For secondary English teachers: in the beginning was the summary.

4. PURPOSE – FACTS

I have mentioned how reductive it can be to narrow texts down according to a single purpose. Every text, to a greater or lesser extent, is persuasive in intent. There might also be shades of advice, explanation and instruction. I find text types and purpose definitions too simplistic. Even gravestones are persuasive texts: they persuade you to consider the person lost.

Learning the difference between fact and opinion is especially important now, given the questionable nature of much of the news we receive. An ability to distinguish between these two elements is one that will reward students in life; consequently, we need to go back to it again and again. They need to be taught how to interrogate facts and opinion and see when writers blend the two or dress the latter as the former. I find teaching the purpose of facts useful. Non-fiction texts often have swathes of facts and spotting these isn't massively helpful, but spotting their purpose is.

- Facts can support or validate the main argument.
- Facts can challenge the reader's opinion.
- Facts can be included to shock.
- Facts can be included to impress.
- Facts can be emotive and create a desired emotion.

In fact, facts (sorry) are rather more versatile than we might immediately imagine and this gives us lots of scope for exploration. Facts are easily visible to students, they often form the backbone of non-fiction texts and their order can be structured for an exact purpose. Why do so many non-fiction texts start with an evocative fact or one designed to shock? It is to provoke a specific reaction from the reader by challenging their assumption of a topic, supporting their way of seeing things or introducing a new way of looking at it.

Each fact can have a different and specific purpose. A fact that challenges a reader's assumptions is intended to cause conflict and antagonism.

Migrant workers pay more tax than the average UK resident.[4]

Nothing causes more antagonism than taxes. Add to that the idea that you are possibly not paying enough tax and you have put red flag to bull.

A fact that supports the reader's view of the world is intended to build a relationship with and connection to the writer. A place of safety, comfort and trust.

Parents now spend less time with their children on average than they did ten years ago.[5]

Most parents, depending on the child, feel guilty about not spending enough time with their offspring. More so if you are a teacher. But a fact like this connects with the reader because it evokes a shared feeling. A feeling common among parents. This fact reassures that they are not alone. They have a friend.

Facts are clear, transparent, structural and, occasionally, emotive. That's why non-fiction writers often leave one fact for the very end. A simple highlighter can help you spot the facts. It helps to remind students that a fact or opinion can be conveyed in

4   This fact is from the Institute of Fake Facts.
5   This fact is from the Department of Misinformation.

just a single word or phrase. They don't just come in little blocks or sentences. They are often blended in to the writing.

From here, students can see the development of the use of facts. Does the text start with a fact? Does it end with one? Facts rarely work on their own. One supports the other. They build on each other to leave the reader with a clear picture or idea. Explore the interconnectivity of the facts and you get to the real purpose of the text.

5. NOUNS, ADJECTIVES AND VERBS

Decluttering a text can help us to explore the meaning and the writer's choices, and having a look at the use of nouns, verbs and adjectives can really unlock things. Here is an extract where Robert Louis Stevenson describes the landscape of the Bay of Monterey in America:

> *These long beaches are enticing to the idle man. It would be hard to find a walk more solitary and at the same time more exciting to the mind. Crowds of ducks and sea-gulls hover over the sea. Sandpipers trot in and out by troops after the retiring waves, trilling together in a chorus of infinitesimal song. Strange sea-tangles, new to the European eye, the bones of whales, or sometimes a whole whale's carcass, white with carrion-gulls and poisoning the wind, lie scattered here and there along the sands. The waves come in slowly, vast and green, curve their translucent necks, and burst with a surprising uproar, that runs, waxing and waning, up and down the long key-board of the beach. The foam of these great ruins mounts in an instant to the ridge of the sand glacis, swiftly fleets back again, and is met and buried by the next breaker. The interest is perpetually fresh. On no other coast that I know shall you enjoy, in calm, sunny weather, such a spectacle of Ocean's greatness, such beauty of changing colour, or such degrees of thunder in the sound. The very air is more than usually salt by this Homeric deep.[6]*

---

6   R. L. Stevenson, The old pacific capital, in *Across the Plains with Other Memories and Essays* (Project Gutenberg ebook edition, 2013 [London: Chatto & Windus, 1915]), pp. 51–71 at p. 51. Available at: https://www.gutenberg.org/files/614/614-h/614-h.htm#page51.

Adjectives	Nouns	Verbs
long	beaches	are
idle	man	would
hard	walk	be
solitary	mind	find
exciting	ducks	hover

When presented with lists like this, students get to see the interconnectivity between words. Taken in isolation, they might begin to notice how very understated the nouns and verbs are. They'd also see how the adjectives are doing most of the work. You could make the linguistic analysis deeper by exploring further sub-categories which the students offer or you might look at the use of determiners, adverbs, etc., but the helpful thing is to see how the language works in isolation. Look at how the adjectives 'long' and 'idle' relate to each other. Can you find any connections between these words? How do these words suggest a sense of peace and simplicity?

There are numerous other activities to do with word lists, such as:

- Produce a new text using these words.

- Pair or group the words.

- Explore alternatives and replace them in the original text.

6. READER AND WRITER RELATIONSHIP – MAKING A DRAMA OF THINGS

Some would say that teaching non-fiction can be ... a little ... dry. Obviously, I disagree with this, but I admit it can be a bit cold, and that's why adding a bit of drama can help. I like getting students to work in pairs for this. One student is the reader, the other is pretending to be the writer (of the text being studied in the lesson). The reader has to explain how they think or feel when reading the text.

I am a bit shocked because ...

I didn't expect ...

I was worried at first that ...

I didn't like ...

At this point, I get students to share their reactions to the text. It does feel like a self-help group and can get a little emotional, but they get the idea really quickly. Either that, or they morph into melodrama in the most unpleasant manner.

Then I get the students to work in pairs again, but this time the writer has to explain what they did and why they wanted the reader to feel a specific emotion.

I wanted you to feel ... so I used ...

I thought you would think ... so therefore ...

I wanted to surprise you, so I ...

The fusion of these two elements helps students to work on the difficult connection between what the reader thinks and feels and the writer's intent, which is a hard thing to develop. And it adds a bit of drama to the lesson.

7. COMPARING TEXTS

There is a danger that we choose binary opposites when we select non-fiction texts for comparison. This is something we'd rarely consider doing with poetry, because we are so clear that poetry is a heavily nuanced and subtle form of writing. We'd happily compare a poem about a garden and a poem about a similar garden from a different poet. We know that no two poets see a garden in the same way. But, when it comes to non-fiction, we go for clear opposites. If a text is talking about how the pay gap between men and women should be reduced then the second text should be from some idiot who thinks it's great as it is, right? By doing that, we reduce complex issues into a simple case of 'for' or 'against' – stark opposites. Ideas are malleable and abstract, so students need to understand that issues, and texts, are not solely one thing or another. They are fully understood in relation to others. To develop students' understanding of perspective, we need to provide them with more points of view and look at the relationship between them. Something we freely do with poetry, yet often shun with non-fiction.

Let's take the topical, or historical depending on when you read this, issue of Britain leaving the European Union. The world would have you think that the issue is a simple case of 'for' or 'against'. Yet on the issue of Brexit there are several different views on the why and why nots. There's the perspective of:

- People who lived in Britain before it joined the European Union.

- People who have only lived in Britain as part of the European Union.

- People who have a family member living in another country within the European Union.

- People whose jobs depend on commerce with countries inside the European Union.

I could go on forever because there are always so many viewpoints on any issue. Through this example we can see historical, conservative, international and local perspectives. Then, you might find a further layer of pessimism, optimism, romanticism, anger, bitterness or resentment under the surface. Each one would have a different, arguably valid, opinion on what should or shouldn't happen. Narrow the exploration to 'for' and 'against' and you cut out points in between. In doing this, you miss the subtle nuances between each line of thought and you narrow your understanding of a complex issue.

The root cause of the problem is our desire to be impartial and show both sides. A common style – which I personally loathe – is discursive writing: turning the world simply into 'for' and 'against'. So, how do we address complexity without this reductionism?

I tend to use a comparative approach:

1   What is your opinion on this topic?

2   What is text A's opinion on this topic?

3   What is text B's opinion on this topic?

4   What is text C's opinion on this topic?

5   What do other people think about this topic?

I build understanding using different opinions on an issue, starting with the students' own. Then, I introduce one text at a time and tease out the connections between them. At the same time, I will see how it links to the students' opinions. Place two texts next to each other and you get a simple spot the difference, but add a third and you start to see the subtle links. You see text A places more emphasis on an aspect which text B is less bothered about, and which text C hasn't even considered worthy of mention. Non-fiction texts are incredibly consumable and we forget that. They are easily digestible and disposable. That's why we shouldn't shy away from using them. Poetry and novels need room to breathe, but non-fiction is tomorrow's chip paper.

English lessons should be about asking the difficult questions. We should be pushing all manner of different perspectives and viewpoints to allow students to form their own. We shouldn't be enforcing a world view of binary opposites but helping them to see the complexity, and to make informed decisions. We need a range of voices in the classroom and it should reflect our democratic principles: everyone has a voice and a vote.

Chapter 6
HOW TO TEACH SHAKESPEARE

I adore teaching the plays of Shakespeare. In fact, I enjoy it so much, I am always on the lookout for opportunities to teach different ones. More has been written about Shakespeare than about any other writer; he deals with complex and shared human experiences which apply to us all. We have all been children. We have all lost something – an object, a pet or a person. We are all hungry for something. His plays are rich in ideas, thought and language. He deals with people in real situations. Soaps spend ages trying to create the level of believability that Shakespeare forges in an hour-and-a-half.

Aside from dealing with complex and emotional experiences, they are also darn good stories which contain challenges to our thinking. What happens when a king goes bad? What happens when a king is killed by his subjects? What happens in a relationship when one person has more power than the other? What happens if you start making decisions based on a prediction of your future?

One of the beauties of the plays is that you can dive in anywhere. You could jump into Benedick and Beatrice's arguing in *Much Ado About Nothing* or explore the opening scene of *Hamlet* and analyse how Shakespeare builds a world through language. There have been countless interpretations and productions, each with a different angle and, like gardening or football, you can either sit on the sidelines watching others or get to the real fun by doing it yourself. Read it aloud. Act it out. Play around with it. The text is malleable and ready for you to shape.

I have had some of my most enjoyable lessons teaching Shakespeare – for example, when working with a Year 10 rugby player pretending to be Lady Macbeth, including blonde wig and high-pitched voice, and when arguments, insightful ones, broke out over whether Shakespeare's portrayal of Shylock is racist or not. Whether it is exploring how Beatrice is the most modern portrayal of a woman in Shakespeare's plays or exploring the use of euphemism, there's so much to take from them. They give so much and they stay with you.

Aside from the cultural angle, there is an even greater argument for studying more and more Shakespeare in the classroom. It shows that you are not willing to patronise students or 'dumb down'. You are giving the students a simple message: you think that they are clever and capable of difficult and great things. Therefore, if a student asks the immortal question, 'Why do we have to learn about Shakespeare?', you may respond with the equally imperishable reply, 'Because the universe says you can't cope with it, but I know you can.'

1. ONE POWERPOINT TO RULE THEM ALL – STRUCTURAL CHOICES

Whether you are looking at language, structure or form, the key thing to explore is why Shakespeare made that specific choice to present his ideas. Teach a student how to spot an oxymoron and you can guarantee they will search for one in every single piece of literature. And that is the problem with Shakespeare. It is all too easy for students to spot devices and forget the big structural choices needed to create a scene.

Take a simple choice like the time of day. What's the impact of this? A scene set during the day might be ordinary, happy, routine, truthful and noisy. A scene set during the night might be unusual, secretive, unhappy, magical and quiet. Take *Macbeth* and the infamous scene after the murder of King Duncan (Act 2, Scene 2). Why set this in the middle of the night? This choice has lots of implications and ramifications:

- Evil spirits are associated with night-time.

- Darkness hides and masks the identity of the culprits.

- Night-time is when we are most vulnerable.

- Night-time is when 'normal' people sleep.

One simple choice has an enormous impact on our experience of the scene and our understanding; it impacts on the staging and the dramatic context, yet students tend towards thinking that noticing an oxymoron is better, perhaps more nuanced, than commenting on the fundamental choice between night and day. There are endless choices to be discussed when looking at scenes: inside or outside, personal or private, social (relating to people and relationships between people) or political (relating to the governing of people), etc. I like to wrap these up in one simple PowerPoint. I use it every time we look at a scene:

What choices has Shakespeare made in this scene?

- inside vs outside

- day vs night

- home vs away

- public vs private

- soliloquy vs dialogue

- action vs inaction

- political vs social vs religious

- men vs women vs men and women

- positive vs negative

- comic vs tragic vs serious

- long vs short

- plot-driven vs not plot-driven

- family vs friends vs enemies vs lovers

- blank verse vs prose vs both

After we have read a scene, I get them to go through the choices made by Shakespeare. Here's an example for the opening scene of *Hamlet*.

---

outside – night – home – public – dialogue – inaction – political – men – negative – serious – long – plot-driven – friends – blank verse

---

Compare that with the opening of *Romeo and Juliet*:

outside – day – away – public – dialogue – action – social – men – negative – tragic – long – plot-driven – enemies – blank verse

It's really very rewarding indeed when students start talking about a scene as being purely plot-driven and, from there, explain how the next is focused on relationship building. All too often, studying a play seems to be about remembering the plot; this approach, however, helps students to explore the important choices and the meaning behind them. When they look at the staging, they see how the plot and subplots link. They see how the use of short, plot-driven scenes speed the play along. They also see how Shakespeare alternates comedic and serious scenes. Choices don't stand alone; for Shakespeare, the pattern or combination creates the desired effect.

Ideally, we want students to see the whole text and the way in which it is structured, and this approach allows them to do this actively as they read. Getting them to see the change from scene to scene is vital. Asking students how this scene differs from the last helps them to see the purpose. As mentioned previously, you sometimes see things in juxtaposition that you miss in isolation.

2. STRUCTURE AND THEMES TOGETHER

Teaching a whole text, for me, is one of the most enjoyable aspects of the job. It can be daunting at first but, after you've cut your teeth on a novel or play once, it gets easier. Each time I study a text with a class, I get something new from it.

One of the main characteristics of Shakespeare's plays is their complexity. The stories are rich and often appear convoluted to the uninitiated. That's the reason I tend to be explicit and upfront about what is happening in the story. For years, I liked to protect the mystery, but it can be quite hard for some students to grasp the plot, especially with the comedies. No matter how much teaching you have about the language, structure and themes, you will struggle to comprehend the text sufficiently to perform a telling analysis on it if you don't have the plot secure in your mind. Consequently, I tell students exactly what happens in a scene before we read it. Take the following example for the opening of *Romeo and Juliet*:

Act 1, Scene 1: Structure

Sampson and Gregory joke.

Fight with Montagues.

Parents arrive.

Prince breaks up fight.

Montague and Benvolio talk about Romeo.

Romeo and Benvolio talk.

This is kept on the board during our reading. Students know what is happening in the scene and it solidifies their understanding so they have a starting point when I ask a question. I will usually use these points as the basis of a quick revision quiz at the start of the next lesson. But it serves a different function too. Take that summary and look at the following questions:

- How does the ending link to the start?
- What pattern is repeated in the scene?
- What changes across the scene?

The interesting thing is that the scene starts and ends with friends talking. But we go from one side of the conflict to the other – the Capulets start, the Montagues finish. The two are clearly defined as opposing sides by the very structure. Shakespeare also takes us from minor to major characters. I love Shakespeare's introduction of characters; it's so very revealing. Shylock is talked about by others before we see him, which suggests his alienation and distance from society; he is a complete outsider. He is talked about and not to. The same happens with Macbeth. Reputation precedes the man in the narrative. Romeo is introduced after we see a series of young men paraded before us. They present a typical view of how men behaved in society at the time: they are impulsive, proud, smutty and occasionally aggressive. Enter Romeo: the complete opposite. When summarised as a list, I find students are able to see structural choices better.

At the same time, I give students a list of themes so that they can link this to the structure:

- love
- hate
- conflict
- death
- destiny
- forgiveness
- family

So students might make the following points:

- The scene starts with hate and ends with love.
- The scene involves several conflicts: physical, emotional, familial, civil.
- Romeo is a symbol of love; the rest of the characters are symbols of hate.
- Family is linked to several aspects: fighting between families, a parent's concern for their child's wellbeing.

Putting the structural summary as a list alongside a list of themes really helps to lift the level of discussion. Students are forced to think about the themes during every scene; they become a constant reference point. By the end of the play, they know the themes extremely well, and they can see how each scene feeds into their overall presentation.

3. DEMYSTIFYING THE LANGUAGE

The hardest part of teaching Shakespeare is the language barrier. There's no getting away from the fact that it is alien to students. You can dress it up and be positive and say that they will understand it in time, but that doesn't really address the problem. One of my favourite lessons involves spelling out why the language is so rich and different and how Shakespeare's plays are scripted so differently to other playwrights'.

The starting point is the context. I get students to imagine a theatrical world without fancy costumes, special effects or stage curtains. Within such a simplified context, what is going to be the most important thing in the play? The answer is usually interesting plots, likeable/dislikeable characters and interesting ideas. Then we explore what you'd do as a playwright to make the audience understand the setting. After a bit of time, we get to the point where they realise that the language would have had a bigger function. It is the reason why all the characters refer to the setting within the dialogue. I rarely enter my house saying, 'I am home and the heating isn't on to protect me from the chill of such a cold night as this.' The language has to set the tone, show the characters' feelings, interest the audience and paint the scene for them. That's why it is so poetic.

At this point, I usually get students to compare the phrase 'I love you' with any romantic monologue from one of Shakespeare's plays. This enables students to see what he is doing. They understand why the language is so detailed. I then get students to construct their own Shakespearean speech. We start off with a simple phrase:

1   Will you marry me?

2   I do not want to be your friend.

3   You are a liar.

4   He is dead.

5   There has been a murder.

In groups or pairs, they have to improve their phrase in a Shakespearian manner. We build it up in stages. After each one, students share their updated version. Take 'You are a liar'.

Stage 1: Pimp up words

You are a deceiver.

Stage 2: A list

You are a cold, callous, careful deceiver.

Stage 3: Body metaphors

You are a cold, callous, careful deceiver whose eyes paint mysteries.

Stage 4: An unusual simile

You are a cold, callous, careful deceiver whose eyes paint mysteries. You smile like a man in death.

Stage 5: Repetition

You are a cold, callous, careful deceiver whose eyes paint mysteries. You smile like a man in death, like a man in life, like a man in doubt.

Stage 6: A reference to a historical event

You are a cold, callous, careful deceiver whose eyes paint mysteries. You smile like a man in death, like a man in life, like a man in doubt. As Cassius once spoke to Caesar's friends, you whisper sweet poison in the ears of others.

Stage 7: A reference to a myth

You are a cold, callous, careful deceiver whose eyes paint mysteries. You smile like a man in death, like a man in life, like a man in doubt. As Cassius once spoke to Caesar's friends, you whisper sweet poison in the ears of others. There's no barrier to your deception, and even Icarus couldn't reach your destiny.

Stage 8: Make it sound Elizabethan

Thou art a cold, callous, careful deceiver whose eyes paint mysteries. Thou smileth like a man in death, like a man in life, like a man in doubt. As Cassius once spoke to Caesar's friends, thine voice whispers sweet poison in the ears of others. There's no barrier to thine deception and even Icarus couldn't reach thine destiny.

OK, it is unlikely to receive any awards, but it gets the message across: Shakespeare's writing is incredibly dense, rich and multilayered. Students assume that you should be able to understand every line instantaneously; in fact, you can't. I often take my Arden version of *Romeo and Juliet* to school and work through it line by line, reading and rereading the text. If we present a simplified solution to reading Shakespeare, we are neglecting the richness of the text. I like using this activity to show them just how deeply rich the writing is, but it also helps students to understand that there are hundreds of references and allusions that they must appreciate in order to grasp the text fully. Spell out the ingredients and students are able to tell if the text needs further unpicking and research.

4. PRONOUNS

Pronouns are incredibly important in any text, yet they are profoundly unsexy and are not things that students pick out of Shakespeare, or indeed any writing. The use of a pronoun can indicate the relationship between characters and whether one likes or dislikes another.

- Does the character refer to them by name or with a pronoun?

- Does the character dehumanise them by using the pronoun 'it' instead of 'he' or 'she'?

- Do they use 'I' to distance themselves from characters or situations or 'we' to be inclusive?

- Do they use the plural 'you' or the singular, more personal 'thou'?

- Do they use the inclusive pronoun 'our' or the individualistic and possessive pronoun 'my'?

The great thing about pronouns is that they tell us about the relationships between, and the thoughts of, characters. And they are easy to identify. A student might not have a good understanding of the Irish Rebellion, but they know a pronoun when they see it – even if they struggle to name it.

Another great concept to teach alongside this is convergence and divergence. We mirror another person's language when we want to be friendly, and we contrast our speech when we want to be distant and polite. How often have we copied a friend's speech pattern in a conversation? And how many parents adopt a telephone voice? Oh, and does that 'posh' telephone voice suddenly evaporate when your mum realises it's her mate Trish from book club on the line?

Getting students to see how characters use pronouns is an important aspect of language analysis in Shakespeare. Here's a small extract from Act 1, Scene 2 of *Julius Caesar*:

CASSIUS *Why, man, he doth bestride the narrow world*

Like a Colossus, and we petty men

Walk under his huge legs and peep about

To find ourselves dishonourable graves.

Men, at some time, are masters of their fates.

The fault, dear Brutus, is not in our stars,

But in ourselves, that we are underlings.

'Brutus' and 'Caesar': what should be in that 'Caesar'?

Why should that name be sounded more than yours?

Write them together: yours is as fair a name;

Sound them, it doth become the mouth as well;

Weigh them, it is as heavy; conjure with 'em,

'Brutus' will start a spirit as soon as 'Caesar'.

Now, in the names of all the gods at once,

Upon what meat doth this our Caesar feed,

That he is grown so great? Age, thou art shamed!

Rome, thou hast lost the breed of noble bloods!

When went there by an age since the Great Flood,

> *But it was famed with more than with one man?*
>
> *When could they say, till now, that talked of Rome,*
>
> *That her wide walks encompassed but one man?*
>
> *Now is it Rome indeed, and room enough,*
>
> *When there is in it but one only man.*
>
> *O, you and I have heard our fathers say*
>
> *There was a Brutus once that would have brooked*
>
> *Th'eternal devil to keep his state in Rome*
>
> *As easily as a king.*

BRUTUS *That <u>you</u> do love <u>me</u>, <u>I</u> am nothing jealous;*

> *What <u>you</u> would work <u>me</u> to, <u>I</u> have some aim.*
>
> *How <u>I</u> have thought of this and of these times,*
>
> *<u>I</u> shall recount hereafter. For this present,*
>
> *<u>I</u> would not so (with love <u>I</u> might entreat <u>you</u>)*
>
> *Be any further moved. What <u>you</u> have said,*
>
> *<u>I</u> will consider; what <u>you</u> have to say,*
>
> *<u>I</u> will with patience hear, and find a time*
>
> *Both meet to hear and answer such high things.*
>
> *Till then, <u>my</u> noble friend, chew upon this:*
>
> *Brutus had rather be a villager*
>
> *Than to repute himself a son of Rome*
>
> *Under these hard conditions as this time*
>
> *Is like to lay upon <u>us</u>.*[1]

---

1   W. Shakespeare, *Julius Caesar* (Ware: Wordsworth Classics, 1992 [1599]), pp. 39–40.

Brutus' use of pronouns compared with Cassius' is interesting. Cassius is trying to persuade Brutus to go against Caesar. Brutus is simply giving his thoughts some words. The use of pronouns shows the relationship between Cassius' and Brutus' feelings, but there is an alternating use of pronouns. We see an emotionally torn Brutus trapped between his thoughts and Cassius' ideas. In the final lines the pronouns are dropped as if Brutus is fed up with this internalised battle; he steps outside himself by referring to himself in the third person instead. Finally, the speech ends with the inclusive 'us', which suggests that he feels a connection with Cassius and isn't distancing himself completely. It could also suggest that Brutus might be coming around to the idea that Caesar needs to be stopped.

Also, Brutus is using the formal version of 'you' as opposed to the more informal 'thou', which indicates that these two are not truly friends or on the same side … yet. There's a level of formality to the relationship. The fact that Brutus mirrors Cassius with formal pronouns shows that they hold the same status. It might also show Cassius' caution. He may be testing the water. He doesn't want to be too close at this stage; he is, after all, suggesting treason to someone close to Caesar. Risky territory.

With pronouns, you can explore how texts are structured and how the characters' thoughts, feelings and motivations change. I'd highly recommend Ben Crystal's work and his Springboard Shakespeare series for a more detailed and precise look at the language choices in Shakespeare's texts. Ben gives teachers and actors a very insightful way into the meaning of some of the subtle choices in the plays.[2]

5. WORDS, WORDS, WORDS

For years, I placed too much emphasis on teaching the 'big guns' of literary analysis, such as simile, metaphor and repetition. You could guarantee that at some point I'd get students to draw the images in a play. I often neglected the simpler words. To be honest, we neglect the simple words in analysis all too often. Students can get a detailed understanding when the focus is narrowed onto one simple word. Take my

---

2   For further examples and explanations see: https://www.shakespeareswords.com/Public/
    LanguageCompanion/ThemesAndTopics.aspx?TopicId=39.

teaching of *A Christmas Carol* and the introduction of the Ghost of Christmas Present. I simply ask students to come up with three reasons for Dickens' choice of the words 'jolly' and 'green'. I present the task like so:

Jolly

Reason 1:

Reason 2:

Reason 3:

Green

Reason 1:

Reason 2:

Reason 3:

The great thing about looking at things like this is that it declutters the thought process and places emphasis on the understandable. Students offer a vast array of ideas. Green could suggest new life, nature or natural experiences. This narrowing of focus really helps to tease out meaning.

I think we underuse students' intuition when it comes to vocabulary. I often ask them to give me the definition of a word. 'Tom, what does the word "jolly" mean?' Tom returns a definition. Making vocabulary a common point of discussion helps maintain an ongoing working knowledge of it. I take issue with teachers providing a glossary for every text studied because it promotes parrot definitions rather than active thinking. I'd rather have students mine their brains than look for the answer in a prepared response. If we don't get students to think about words, then we are not getting them to explore meaning. If we don't get students to actively construct definitions, then how are we going to get them to read independently?

Let's go back to the exchange between Cassius and Brutus. Cassius uses the word 'breed' when persuading Brutus to consider his position in relation to Caesar. Brutus, in response, uses the word 'villager' when considering what Cassius has said to him.

Breed

Reason 1: controlled selection of the family line.

Reason 2: superiority in relation to others.

Reason 3: without imperfections or weaknesses.

Villager

Reason 1: an insult.

Reason 2: something basic/not sophisticated – would rather make sacrifices than live in these conditions.

Reason 3: Brutus wants to distance himself – clear division between city of Rome and village.

There are hundreds of possible reasons for Shakespeare putting these words in the mouths of these characters. Here we see the class issues and the 'them' and 'us' attitude of the noblemen of Rome – their attitude to class is bubbling under the surface.

In addition to narrowing the focus down to single words, I teach students to learn single-word quotations about characters. This approach has been far more effective than learning large swathes of text. Recalling that Romeo is referred to as a 'lamb' and 'effeminate' has helped my students structure decent arguments when exploring the role of masculinity in *Romeo and Juliet*.

Finally, one last thing to do with a single word: get students to write a paragraph on a single word choice. Believe me, the results are interesting, developed and detailed. Write one paragraph explaining why Dickens used 'Twist' as a surname for Oliver. If students start with a word, they often produce some of their best answers. They have a focus but they can bring in other literary devices and link those to that original word.

6. PREDICTING HOW SHAKESPEARE WILL WRITE – THINK LIKE A PLAYWRIGHT

Every child is a wannabe playwright, poet and author. Every child has this potential. An underestimated question in the classroom is, 'What would you do in the writer's shoes?' We ask students to predict what will happen in the plot, yet we rarely ask them what they'd write. I think every English teacher has had to deal with a student asking if Shakespeare really intended to do something or not. Unless we are able to conduct a successful seance, we will never know. So we guess. But we try to make our guesses intelligent.

Take the following situation: a teenage girl falls in love with a boy from a family that her own despises. No guesses where it is from. *EastEnders*. Only joking. It is the premise of *Romeo and Juliet*. Ask a student, 'How would you introduce such a story to an audience?' They enjoy coming up with ideas. It's a natural human trait which is undervalued in the classroom.

They might come up with ideas like:

- Start with the girl – build the relationship up with her. We identify with her as the protagonist and see her fall for this boy from the wrong family.

- Start with the boy – build the relationship up with him. We identify with him as the protagonist and see him fall for this girl.

- Start with the parents – show how controlling and powerful they are – they come first.

Students present their options and evaluate the best approach. When presented with the playwright's choice, they can understand why the final version was chosen over the others. Then throw in the fact that Shakespeare starts the story by giving a plot overview in the prologue and then writes a scene featuring the parents, followed by the introduction of Romeo. Why would you make that choice as a playwright?

Two households, both alike in dignity

(In fair Verona, where we lay our scene),

From ancient grudge break to new mutiny,

Where civil blood makes civil hands unclean.

From forth the fatal loins of these two foes,

A pair of star-crossed lovers take their life:

Whose misadventured piteous overthrows

Doth with their death bury their parents' strife.

The fearful passage of their death-marked love,

And the continuance of their parents' rage,

Which, but their children's end, nought could remove,

Is now the two hours' traffic of our stage;

The which, if you with patient ears attend,

What here shall miss, our toil shall strive to mend.[3]

Why start with the boy first? Why not with the girl? It is better to start with a list of possibilities than explore one choice in isolation. Evaluation is deemed a high-level skill, yet you need to see how choices relate in order to evaluate properly. This approach allows you to do that.

Another approach I use involves providing alternatives. These are some of the choices I'd explore with the prologue:

- reveal the ending vs don't reveal the ending

- teenagers vs adults

- fight between two families vs fight between two countries

- sad introduction vs happy introduction

- a small speech vs characters talking to each other

- refers to death vs refers only to love

---

3   W. Shakespeare, *Romeo and Juliet* (Ware: Wordsworth Classics, 1992 [1595]), p. 35.

The students are provided with this list of choices, and they have to discuss why Shakespeare went with the choice underlined instead of the other option. The beauty of this approach is that it forces students to discuss the reasoning behind a specific choice. They might explore how revealing the ending creates a sense of expectation or narrative drive to the story; we know how the story ends, but we don't how it gets to that point. They might also explore how a sense of doom touches every action, or inaction, in the play, making the audience ponder what the fatal cause of their untimely demise is; their lives are now soaked in misery, making any happiness bittersweet.

The next step is to get students to think of another possibility for each one. Shakespeare chose *teenagers* and not adults, but what could his third option be? Fairies? Animals? Pensioners? Each option considered helps students to understand why the original decision was made. If fairies or animals were chosen, then we'd lose a sense of realism. Therefore, Shakespeare may have been wanting to create a realistic, relatable and common experience for the audience rather than a playful and unrealistic one. But, of course, we know Shakespeare was retelling an already popular story and that the choice in question wasn't his own. Through comparisons students are able to explore meaning, which is very hard to do when exploring a writer's decisions in isolation.

7. CONTEXT

Context is a tricky aspect to teach as students easily slip into chucking in (cutting and pasting) large pieces of information. Essays can become a list of regurgitated facts. I find the teaching of context is, therefore, best served by keeping the information concise. If students are limited to the short piece of contextual information you've provided, they have to work hard to explain its relevance. Below is a list I often use with Years 10 and 11 when teaching *Romeo and Juliet*.

Women in 1595

- Women had no power and were reliant on their fathers and husbands for all necessities. They were the property of the men, who could do what they liked with them; women <u>belonged</u> to men.

- Women couldn't own <u>property</u>.

- Queen Elizabeth I did not marry for fear a man would have more <u>power</u> than her.

- Women could not <u>vote</u>.

- Women had no legal <u>rights</u>.

- Women were <u>never schooled</u>. Education was seen as unnecessary and pointless for women.

- A woman's <u>only role</u> in society was to marry. This was organised by her father.

- Marriages tended to be based around <u>financial security</u>. Love wasn't necessarily a deciding factor. Marriage helped the male's family secure money through a dowry or helped to build <u>alliances</u> and profitable connections between families.

- Marriage from the age of <u>12</u> was acceptable. This was more common in rich families than in poor families.

The key words are underlined – these are the linking points. Students have to remember these words only – belonged, property, power, vote, rights, never schooled, only role, financial security, alliances and 12. The words become sticking points to screw their courage, I mean ideas, to.

Lady Capulet therefore plays a minor role in the play as her station in life was solely to support her husband. Her interactions on stage are only in relation to her role in the marriage – which was to do Capulet's bidding.

The less contextual information you give, the more the students have to work on embellishing it. By this I mean keep the individual points short rather than reduce the volume of ideas. I tend to repeat these facts and regularly set them as questions. What does age 12 signify for a female? Another approach to teaching context is

158

simply to look at areas of difference. A nice way to do this is with a little grid which students use to explore how each aspect is different to the present.

The Elizabethan view of society

What was the Elizabethan view of ...?

Men	
Women	
Family	
Children	
Marriage	
Love	
Law/Rules	
Class	
Authority	

Power	
Rich/Poor	
Strength/Weakness	
Work	
Youth/Old age	
Religion	
Hate	
Violence	
Respect	

Getting students to see that the rules of life can be different during different periods of time is important, though the similarities are important too. Take gender in *Romeo and Juliet*. Students might come up with the following points:

- Men were quick to fight and use force if necessary.

- Men liked to wind people up.

- Men were worried about losing respect or being publicly embarrassed.

- Men tended to focus on sexual relations rather than love.

- Men were distant from their parents.

Now that we have a set of statements based on the play, students can discuss whether that element or characteristic has increased or decreased over time. Shakespeare was writing about the human condition, so the experiences are similar to today's, but may have changed perspective. Take the 'men were quick to fight' statement. That might be true nowadays, but it is probably less common and would now, more often than not, be fuelled by alcohol.

Context isn't solely about facts. It is about ideas too. The problem students have is that the past and the present can be seen as binary opposites. But there were men, women, marriages, old and young people in the past and, heavens, they exist in the present too. It is more important to see how men have changed and how they have not. What has changed are the social rules. Humans aren't fundamentally different, they are just living by a different set of rules.

Teach students the rules governing a society. Take the following ideas about class in Edwardian Britain in *An Inspector Calls*.

- A poor person has no manners/class/sophistication/education.

- A poor person can never become wealthy.

- The poor and the rich should never mix – in friendships/relationships/work.

- A poor person should be grateful for what the rich provide them.

- The rich don't want to see or hear the poor; they just need them to do a job.

- The rich employ the poor.

- A rich person can sack or punish a poor employee without consequences.

Understanding the rules of an age is incredibly important for understanding the context. The class system is evident in all British texts to some level. So too is the

American Dream in the work of American writers. Both are notions that govern the ways in which people work, act, think and believe. But, like all rules, there's always someone willing to defy them. When teaching context, it is helpful to use phrases like 'majority' and 'minority' so that you can get across to students that not everybody followed the rules, and when they didn't, this led to social change. Additionally, it is important to refer to 'shades' and 'continuums' because nothing is ever consistent, constant, clear or concrete. Masculinity is a continuum and Tybalt and Romeo are at opposite ends of it at the start of the play.

Chapter 7
HOW TO TEACH STUDENTS TO ANALYSE TEXTS EFFECTIVELY

Textual analysis is a staple of most English lessons. The surprising thing is that I don't recall many of the ones I had as a student focusing on the analysis of a text. I studied poems and novels, but I just don't think that the analysis of texts was at the forefront of English teaching at that time. The focus was on stories and ideas, and writing skills were the driving force back then.

The English classroom of today contains so much analysis that maybe we've gone too far the other way. The insistence on finding a simile and an obscure piece of rhetoric in the text has meant that ideas, thinking, appreciation and joy have been neglected because they get in the way of spotting techniques. The latter has made English a more concrete subject. For years, we struggled with it being abstract. How many times have I faced a parent telling me that their child, usually a boy, prefers maths and science? They inform me that he has a factual mind. I generally read that as 'he can't be bothered to write and has little imagination'.

Spotting words and techniques does not analysis make, however. There is so much more behind a single word or simile: thoughts, ideas, philosophies, politics, issues, problems and religions. Neglect the abstract and you'll have students underperforming in the subject. Analysis is the fusion of the concrete with the abstract.

What came first: the thought or the technique? Of course, thought came first and then man invented writing to communicate thought to a wider audience. I think there should be a greater emphasis on ideas and thoughts in the classroom. English lessons shouldn't be shackled slave-like to a curriculum. They should dance, skip and pirouette from one large idea to the next. The only time when we touch earth is when we look at the texts. It's our duty to balance analysis with new ideas and new thinking. I want students to leave my classroom able to communicate sophisticated ideas and thoughts clearly. They might never have to spot a simile again in their life, but they will be able to express a point on Facebook, and at least they'll be using the appropriate version of 'there/they're/their' (I hope) and considering whether they can be bothered to add punctuation.

1. MULTIPLE-CHOICE ANALYSIS

One of the hardest things in English is getting students to form ideas and opinions independently. Even though teenagers have tons of opinions on a select range of topics, when faced with a text they can struggle to form them. As teachers, we know that students *are* capable but there's often a hidden, secret barrier preventing them. Therefore, when faced with a struggling class, I use this little approach.

First, I give them a quote from the text. In this case, *Great Expectations*.

> *I saw that the bride within the bridal dress had withered like the dress, and like the flowers, and had no brightness left but the brightness of her sunken eyes.*[1]

Then I give students four possible interpretations. To help them, I might throw in a silly one. They discuss which one bests describes the text.

1 Flowers are symbols of life, and withered flowers show a lack of life and possibly death.	2 We associate light with life, and when a light dies we think of death or something bad.	3 Flowers are pretty and, as they wither, they become ugly, like the woman.	4 She used to be beautiful, but age has changed her and she is half the person she used to be.

---

1   C. Dickens, *Great Expectations* (Project Gutenberg ebook edition, 2008 [1867]), ch 8. Available at: http://www.gutenberg.org/files/1400/1400-h/1400-h.htm.

Admittedly, there is often a slow warm-up before we get to high-level thinking. This is a shortcut that looks at symbolism early. It models analytical thought processes and shows what sort of things students should be thinking. They see what they could *possibly* say. It makes the abstract concrete. The next stage is to get them to pick their own quotations and construct four interpretations for each one. I really like this approach as it shows students that there isn't just one answer: a common misunderstanding. We are not maths and science – there are no right or wrong answers in English, just better explanations.

Plus, there's loads of fun to be had in making up silly interpretations. Did you know that Dickens might have named Miss Havisham after Hovis bread as he wanted to highlight her obsession with it? This isn't true, of course, but it gets students to explore the choice of her name and to evaluate and justify possible interpretations.

2. ADVERBS FOR EVALUATING AND ANALYSING

When students are stuck with a text, their default method can be to retell the story instead of analyse it. This would be comical if it didn't cost them quite so many marks in the exam. Hey, examiner, I don't think you know the book you are testing me on, so I am going to tell you what happens in *A Christmas Carol*, just in case you haven't read it. The journey from retelling to analysing is a difficult one. One thing I do to guide students is look at the use of specific adverbs:

- surprisingly

- typically

- stereotypically

- realistically

- unrealistically

- convincingly

- unconvincingly

Adverbs help students to communicate the impact on the reader.

Surprisingly, Dickens starts the story with the death of a minor character, Jacob Marley.

Unrealistically, Shakespeare suggests to us that Romeo falls in love immediately.

These adverbs perform an important job in the analysis, and I do think it is incredibly useful to signpost it.

The writer is going against convention.

Surprisingly, Dickens presents the poor in both a positive and a negative light.

The writer is doing what most writers would do in this situation.

Typically, Shakespeare uses the male characters to initiate conflict and tension in the opening of the play.

The writer is doing the most obvious thing.

Stereotypically, Priestley links capitalism with arrogance, superiority and elitism.

The writer is aiming for realism.

Realistically, Steinbeck presents the relationship between Lennie and George as both cruel and loving.

The writer might be trying to make things realistic but doesn't achieve it.

Unrealistically, Susan Hill uses the dog, Spider, as a replacement for a supporting character in The Woman in Black.

The writer is completely achieving an effect.

Convincingly, Robert Louis Stevenson makes us warm to the character of Long John Silver at the start of Treasure Island.

The writer is failing to achieve an effect.

Unconvincingly, Golding uses a lack of identification of dialogue in Lord of the Flies *to convey the confusion and chaos of the situation.*

As with all things to do with analysis, it is the explanation that's important. Let's not fool ourselves that one simple adverb will transform a student's writing. That's why it is so important to get students to explain their responses.

Surprisingly, Dickens starts the story with the death of a minor character, Jacob Marley. We'd normally expect the protagonist to be the main focus of an opening. However, Dickens focuses first on Jacob Marley to symbolise what Scrooge might become and also to explain Scrooge's current emotional and physical state.

Unrealistically, Shakespeare suggests to us that Romeo falls in love immediately. The playwright is suggesting how the young confuse initial physical attraction with love. It is more common for people to fall in love after spending some time together.

3. INTERPRETATIONS

Teachers are pressed for time and, sadly, this means that we don't have sufficient hours to allow for much organic analysis in class. I could spend years reading *Romeo and Juliet*, for example, and tease out so much from it that I'd never want to stop. But this is unlikely to be allowed. For some time now, I've topped up students' knowledge of a text by providing my own interpretations. Take the following for *An Inspector Calls*:

Mrs Birling

- Highlights how women didn't always sympathise with other women.

- Shows how people only care for their family and their reputation.

- Shows how people are only kind and charitable when it suits them.

- Shows how women abused their power too.

- Gives the audience an idea of what Sheila could become.

- Shows how inequality was caused by both genders – not just by men treating women badly.

When we have covered the content and are preparing for the exam, I provide students with a range of interpretations to give them what Andy Tharby describes as a 'bedrock of knowledge'.[2] Yes, students could come to these interpretations on their own, but often the pace of this is not conducive to learning or to the progress of the class. A bank of interpretations helps them to form new ideas. The less able students latch on to the idea and regurgitate it while the more able find that they don't quite fit with what they want to say and so adapt them, developing a new interpretation. A bit like the concept of core knowledge (that basic information you need to grasp in order to access a topic), students need core interpretations. It is important they know that Mr Birling is a symbol of capitalism. When they have that core interpretation, they can develop others, such as:

- There are characters whose lives benefit from capitalism.

- There are characters whose lives are negatively affected by capitalism.

- There are characters who are the opposite of capitalism.

- There are characters who show us different types of capitalism.

When you know that Mr Birling is a symbol of capitalism, you can then interpret that Eva Smith is the collateral damage caused by the machine. Ideas don't sit in the brain alone and, when placed together or in proximity, they can generate interesting and thoughtful new shoots. However, without the core knowledge or a rudimentary interpretation, students will not get further than the plot. They need something to metaphorically light the blue touch paper of original thought, but often that

---

2   A. Tharby, English teaching and the problem with knowledge, *Reflecting English* [blog] (26 October 2014). Available at: https://reflectingenglish.wordpress.com/2014/10/26/english-teaching-and-the-problem-with-knowledge/.

something is someone else's thought. Therefore, I test and revise core interpretations. We can never know what the exam questions will be, so there is value in teaching interpretations based on several different elements of a text.[3]

4. USE OF QUOTATIONS

Using quotations is a requirement in all GCSE English exams and rightly so. A quotation is a thing of beauty and is so versatile. There's so much teachers can do with them in a lesson: we can analyse in great detail, or we can link to the broader text. Closed-book exams have placed a greater emphasis on knowing texts and memorising large swathes of quotations. But memory is finite and subjects are vying for available brain space, so I tend to place a lot of emphasis on learning single-word quotations. After studying lots of exam papers, you notice that the best students use lots of single-word quotations rather than longer ones.

Take the following words used to describe Romeo:

- pilgrim
- villain
- young
- madman
- rose
- waverer
- lamb
- effeminate
- sweet

---

3   I have placed a number of these interpretation lists on my blog, which you are welcome to use. C. Curtis, Revision cards, *Learning from My Mistakes* [blog] (4 January 2018). Available at: http://learningfrommymistakesenglish.blogspot.co.uk/2018/01/revision-cards.html.

I get students to memorise these because they serve so many functions, for example:

1   Analyse specific language.

Lamb – the noun reflects his inexperience and the fact that he hasn't yet reached adulthood. It also reflects his lack of strength and experience.

2   Link ideas across the text and spot patterns.

Rose – links to the use of garden imagery with the friar's garden and Capulet's reference to Juliet as a 'bud'.

3   Highlight a character's attitude to a subject.

Effeminate – highlights Romeo's realisation that love has changed him and his arguably sexist attitude.

The great thing is that each word is loaded and has so many uses. I find, as Mark Roberts has in his blog post on one-word retrieval practice,[4] that looking at words changes how you teach because you begin to collect word banks and expand the students' repertoire of quotes. You can also track the development of character through the use of three words.

Take Scrooge in *A Christmas Carol*:

oyster – ogre – friend

The words used here quite obviously show us how the character develops and changes. However, some of the words selected might allow a more subtle interpretation. Students can easily explain how Scrooge is an oyster at the start. Then they can continue the imagery when they say that by the end of the story Scrooge opens

---

4   M. Roberts, A quick word retrieval practice for single word quotations, *Mark Roberts Teach* [blog] (25 November 2017). Available at: https://markrobertsteach.wordpress.com/2017/11/25/a-quick-word-retrieval-practice-for-single-word-quotations/.

up and shares his pearl (wealth) and, as a result, becomes a friend to Bob Cratchit. Simply put, from single words students can make connections across the whole text. So much meaning can be squeezed out of a word. Give it a go. How much can you say about the word 'serpent' when used to describe Romeo?

5. TONE AND VOICE IN ESSAY WRITING

As mentioned previously, essay writing is perceived as being less interesting than creative writing. I know a lot of teachers who'd rather ask students to write a story than get them to write an analytical essay, and you can see why. Essay writing seems a bit dry – like eating a slice of bread without butter or jam. And it can be hard to challenge that notion.

The problem is with the tone and voice that we assume an analytical essay needs. A voice that sounds like a trainspotter. It lacks emotion and feeling: 'It is a commonly held fact that the 8.15 from Manchester is regularly on time.' The problem is that the perception is one of two extremes and the alternative reads like a children's TV presenter: 'Oh my goodness! That funny Dickens! He certainly knows how to fool the reader, because he had us all fooled for a bit, didn't he?'

I believe English teachers should have a bookcase full of essays. Read them and use them in lessons because they are often far from dry. They are formal, but they have a voice and are often as witty as they are learned. Take any bright student and read their essays. They have a voice and their tone varies. It might be subtle and slight, but it is there.

Show students that the tone of essays can be flattering, comical, serious, shocking or ironic. Subtly and understatedly so, but those thoughts are there. The one thing we want to avoid is informality. You can have a voice in essay writing, but you want the right level of formality. Moving from using personal pronouns to the impersonal variety or the passive voice helps to get the ball rolling.

_I_ _think Shakespeare is highlighting how parents are unable to control their children._

_It_ _can be seen that Shakespeare is highlighting how parents are unable to control their children._

An extension of this is replacing pronouns with nouns like 'the reader', 'experts', 'the audience', 'critics' or 'feminists'. It is all too easy for students to use 'you' and 'we', which again makes for a personal and informal read.

The audience _sees that Shakespeare is highlighting how parents are unable to control their children._

This demonstrates clearly that the writer is somehow separate to the audience and possibly to the idea. Phrases like 'audiences feel' and 'critics say' give students a starting point to expand on or challenge an opinion. Even the nouns used to describe the writer help to aid meaning in an essay. It is at times comical and infuriating when students refer to writers by their first names. As I say to students, unless you have had them buy you a drink in a pub, never refer to the writer by their first name. Teaching students to vary how they refer to writers is important as it aids cohesion and avoids repetition. Teach students to avoid endlessly repeating 'writer'; alternatives such as _author_, _Dickens_ and _he_ allow for variety and subtle cohesion across a paragraph and an essay. A student's essay writing voice is just as important as their understanding of the writer's. We are just looking at using language differently in a particular context.

6. FORMING AN OPINION – TALKING IN LESSONS

Before we learned to write, we spoke. Before students write about an idea, they should have the opportunity to talk it through. The balance between speech and writing in the classroom is difficult, of course. Too much talking sounds like students are doing very little work. Too much writing sounds like the teacher is Gradgrindian. The classroom is the training room. We are training students for exams and, more importantly, for real life, so it is important that we train them to discuss ideas. It's a sad fact that discussion around the dining room table is a rarity for a lot of students nowadays. You only have to see a modern family at mealtimes. The challenge is to see who can avoid communication and eye contact the most. Social media allows people to express a point but not actually discuss an idea. That's perhaps why trolling has become so prevalent; it is easy to express thoughts dogmatically. But ideas need discussing, shaping, moulding and shaving. Everybody and anybody can have an opinion; it is the intelligent ones who have evidenced and explored it, considering the alternatives.

A colleague of mine used to start discussions from a negative standpoint. She'd say to the class: 'Right, convince me that you are not all bigots.' The great thing about this statement was that it made them defensive from the off. They had to explore justifications and express passionate opinions. We shouldn't shy away from discussing difficult topics or ideas. If we do, then bigotries and misconceptions can remain intact and problematic views can fester and develop. Isn't it better to talk about things? Recently, I have been addressing how girls accept low-level sexism in the classroom because it is seen as a compliment or banter. The classroom is a safe space and a negotiating table for the discussion of these ideas.

Place ideas at the centre of lessons. Collect them. List them. Take the following relating to the presentation of women in *Macbeth*:

- Women are more intelligent than men.

- Men are physically strong, but women are emotionally stronger.

- Men have reason to not trust women.

- Women see the bigger picture and men only see what is relevant to them.

A list of ideas often makes a better starting point than the text itself does. Students can openly discuss these statements without knowing much about *Macbeth*. They are universal ideas about the 'real world'. Some may be correct. Some are probably incorrect. But they all provoke discussion. Teenagers can spew forth their ideas on how males are emotionally stronger than females or how females are untrustworthy. The turning point is linking the idea to the text.

We want students to generate ideas on their own, but they won't be able to create them from a vacuum. That's why every lesson should focus on generating ideas, no matter how small or large. The English classroom can react to what is in the news that day: there are always ideas floating in the atmosphere. Take the election of Donald Trump. One of the many worms the opening of this can revealed was the debate about men and women in politics – especially regarding how men treat women. Some ideas are difficult, unpleasant or uncomfortable, but we patronise students if we don't give them a chance to talk about them. Most problems can be resolved with talk, and we should use our classrooms to model this. The classroom should be a symposium of thought and not the closeted, scripted bubble of an Orwellian overlord.

7. MODEL THINKING

Our thought processes are internalised so we need to be explicit about them, or they seem a magical mystery to students. Possibly we should be pantomime in our approach. Now, where is that quotation? It's behind you.

How do I model the thinking? There are several ways:

1   **My thinking monologue.** I talk while I write and, with the aid of a PowerPoint or a visualiser, I show students what I've written.

The question is asking me to look at the presentation of women, but I think the story is more interested in how women behave towards men, so I think I must also look at the way men are presented, and I'll use them in the comparison. Now, I am going to start with my theory. William Shakespeare presents women as a binary of weak and strong in Much Ado About Nothing *yet presents men as equal.*

Of course, sir sounds like a nutcase, but he is showcasing the way in which we think. We don't really think in a logical sequence. We jump, skip, flip and backflip between disparate ideas. Mid-sentence we'll have a brainwave or find that one sentence jogs something else three paragraphs back. We all accept the stream of consciousness narrative in fiction, yet we promote a rigid, logical and chronological order when exploring the thought processes involved in analytical writing.

2   **Ask the audience** – a collective approach to writing. You write on the board and metaphorically phone a friend for ideas.

Look! I have used the word 'weak' twice in this sentence – can anybody think of a different word I could use instead?

The key thing is getting students to write out the paragraphs when you've completed them. The main reason for this is muscle memory and practice. How can we expect students to develop their proficiency at analysing text if they aren't getting used to writing in this style? Plus, it means students will have an example to refer to.

3   **Model with concrete examples.**

I am forever photocopying good examples of students' work. I have a folder full of them and use them all the time. Give the class an example and get them to write in that style about their text. A lot of time is spent on sentence starters but, actually, what is more important is the expression and construction of an idea. I have seen endless sheets of connectives or discourse markers and all they do is ensure students use plenty of connectives – much like how people use fairy lights on their house at Christmas, it ends up in a gaudy mess. Students use them without care or consideration. A good analytical paragraph will probably only use one discourse marker and that will often be the word 'however'. Some paragraphs will not have any explicit markers. Not every paragraph needs to start with a connective and it is rare that they should. Ideas need to breathe and they can't if a student is continually flipping between different ones because the teacher has advised them to pepper their essay with subordinating conjunctions.

Give students an example and get them to emulate it. The end result will have to be independent, but the journey can be supported in a number of ways. An example of the style to follow can be better than a set formula. A student can then copy words, phrases, lines or sentence constructions rather than using a word list. An example shows context. They see how different constructions link to the surrounding words and how they fit in with the syntax and the flow of ideas. All too often, students use a phrase like 'on the other hand' when there hasn't been a first hand to start with: it was on a list. Writing isn't as simple as we try to make it seem. Just add a word here and it will be good. Just use a PEE paragraph and you'll analyse in detail. This isn't the case. Writing is far more complex than we'd like to believe and students need to see examples in order to emulate them.

4   Do it in steps.

a   **What is your idea?** Students write a sentence.

b   **How does the writer show this?** Students write down a piece of evidence, such as a quotation or an example from the text.

c   **Why does the writer do this?** Students write down an explanation of their idea.

This is how it looks.

What is your idea?

Charles Dickens explores how we aren't born cruel but the experiences we have in life teach us to be cruel.

How does the writer show this?

Through the characters of Fred and Scrooge.

176

Why does the writer do this?

Dickens uses the contrast between the characters to highlight that it isn't natural for Ebenezer Scrooge to be unkind; his nephew is a kind, warm-hearted character, suggesting to us that cruelty isn't in the family's nature. Scrooge became cruel as a result of his experiences rather than it being a natural part of him. This provides us with a sense of hope for Scrooge to be redeemed: negative experiences have made him cruel, so positive experiences may make him kind.

This is an approach I have borrowed from Louisa Enstone.[5] She uses this instead of the dreaded PEE structure and, for me, it works much better with less able writers. There are various ways to do this, and it can be easily adapted for students' different needs. Students can be given the *what* as a ready-made sentence and they have to find the *how* and the *why*.

Shakespeare presents love as undefinable and constantly changing.

Shakespeare presents parents as rigid and unmoveable in the play.

Shakespeare presents adults as people governed by their selfish needs rather than the desire to make a better world.

Another way to do this is to provide students with several different, disconnected examples of whats, hows and whys and they have to match up the correct ones.

---

5   Find her on Twitter @englishlulu.

Chapter 8
HOW TO TEACH ACCURACY

Accuracy is simple thing in the classroom: we all want students to produce accurate pieces of writing. But there needs to be a balancing act for the teacher. The expectation that every inaccuracy is picked up and corrected is a ridiculous notion to many, yet I've seen leadership teams insist upon it. Thirty students produce a stadium full of errors daily and it is a constant firefight. If a teacher spent the whole lesson addressing inaccuracies, they'd never get through any content. Therefore, I tend to walk around the class and read work over the student's shoulder. With a pen, I will circle an error. Then I see if the student self-corrects the error. If they don't correct it automatically, I talk them through the error. Common errors are discussed with the whole class. Accuracy needs to be a daily habit and routine for all.

To start off with, the English language is full of irregular spellings. When you have a language that is made up of German, Latin, French and various other languages, you have multiple rules and we have incorporated irregular foreign spelling patterns as we've assimilated words. Some argue that we'd be in a better place if we enforced a standardised way of spelling, but that would be like trying to wrangle a bag of snakes.

I am a big believer in systematic exposure to spelling. We have a weekly spelling test; students have the list in advance and are expected to systematically learn the words. Each year group has a distinct list. And I highlight any particular spelling errors in students' work.

Why do students struggle with accuracy? Aside from some who have genuine cognitive wiring issues, we can usually put students into three behavioural camps: the 'haven't been taught' group, the 'blindness' group and the 'lazy' group. I'll address dyslexic students later and I obviously exclude them from the above categories. I have two daughters and, like all good teachers, observe how my children learn. One is a great speller, but she can be lazy so will get the occasional word wrong. The other rushes to get her ideas on the page so quickly that there are always several mistakes. When questioned, one can see the mistakes and the other can't and needs directing to them. One child is lazy with spellings. The other is blind to them. It's interesting as they are identical twins. Maybe there is something about their home environment … The classroom is where we should be addressing both laziness and blindness. What am I doing as a teacher to address the lazy spellers? What am I doing to address the blind spellers?

There are some students who struggle with spellings and spotting errors because the writing is hard to decode, and I empathise with them. But not every student who cannot spell is dyslexic and it is unfair to dyslexic students if that myth is propagated by teachers. Although everybody is on a spectrum, dyslexia is a complex issue and there is more to it than just spelling. If a parent raises a concern about their child, point them in the direction of the teacher in charge of special educational needs (SEN). Spelling is a small part of dyslexia, but it isn't the one and only marker. And we need to be careful of pronouncing every child who can't spell or who mistakes b's for d's a dyslexic student. A label can help support a child, but an incorrect label can be a shield to hide behind, stopping the real issue from being fixed.

Accuracy should be the classroom's air freshener. You might need it more sometimes, especially after Year 9 PE, or you might turn it down occasionally if it risks becoming overpowering, but it is always there. In some form. In some manner. In some way.

1. SPELLING – THREE CHOICES

One solution for spellings puts the emphasis back on the students. Over time, they have slowly learned to ignore it, or they constantly ask teachers how to spell a word even when the dictionary is right next to them on the desk. Instead, this strategy plays an active role in helping them get better and also addresses the error blindness I mentioned before. They take a bit more responsibility for their spellings.

First, the student identifies the word they struggle to spell – this can be done during or after writing. Then, on a scrap bit of paper, the student writes down three possible ways to spell the word.

implys   implies   implis

The student then looks at the three alternatives and decides which one looks right. More often than not they select the right one. I've seen students improve their spelling overnight with this approach. It doesn't work for students with poor visual memory, however, but it does help some. Often, students think that spelling needs to be an automated or quick process and they don't like using a dictionary because it slows them down when they want to be seen to keep up with the rest of the class. This approach allows them to do things quickly and save face in the classroom.

2. DRAFT IN THREES

I love drafting in lessons. Mainly because there is less lesson to plan, but also because it gets you to the heart of the writing process and the problems students have with specific parts. I will often insist they draft in threes.

Draft 1: will check they understand the task.

Draft 2: will check that they have addressed any writing issues.

Draft 3: will be the polish.

I think the repeated process is really handy because each draft is flagged as a different task, and it has a different impact on different students. The good writers use the drafting process to refine and hone their work and the weak writers make large leaps in progress – draft 1 contains no punctuation whereas draft 2 contains some secure use. As I've alluded to, writing is hard. Students get things wrong. It may seem that punctuation, for example, is obvious but 11-year-olds can get so involved in the moment and in their ideas that they forget about its existence.

I like to simplify the marking sometimes and use a mark out of 10. Take this example for a student writing a paragraph of a horror story:

Draft 1: 3/10

Target: Add more ambitious and effective vocabulary.

Draft 2: 7/10

Target: Vary how you structure your sentences.

Draft 3: 9/10

Target: Be more creative with how you present your ideas – steal ideas from the examples in the lesson.

This example shows improvement as a process and it teaches students to see it as such. All too often, writing is seen as merely the *product* of learning, as a form of communication that happens when it is assessment time. Drafting several times is really helpful to me and to the students. You see the students who don't listen and who will not make progress. You see the impact of your instructions. You note that there are students who don't follow instructions. Using this approach throughout Key Stage 3 helps students to develop their writing 'muscle memory' in preparation for exam season, when time for planning is more limited.

3. REFUSAL

Just say no. I often tell students that I am not going to mark a piece of work. Students need to know that we have high expectations of them. If I mark a piece of work that doesn't use punctuation, it tells them that they can hand it in like this again. It is amazing how much of an impact you get from telling a student that you are not going to mark their work until they have done X or Y. We must articulate when effort or attention to detail is not good enough. A lack of care shows a lack of respect. The student should be working harder than the teacher.

I always think that the way we respond to work is important; praise everything and we devalue both the work and praise itself. I tend towards being sparse with praise. Regarding the effort put into a piece of work, praise should be worked for and punishment must be clear. Refusing to mark or read something until the student has done a bit more work sends a message: I think you are capable of more.

4. HOMEWORK – LISTS

We try to help students improve their spellings in lessons, but for the student this is often a passive process. They are dependent on the teacher and expecting a magical external cure for their spelling affliction. I like to make students take responsibility. In addition to a regular list of spellings, I get students to write down each mistake they make.

We all know the importance of repetition, but there's more we can do to support their spelling. I give students a blank sheet of paper and get them to write down their frequent spelling errors. This can be done as a booklet or a bookmark, anything really. The student can then use this as an aide-memoire. Instead of digging deep into the recesses of their brain, they can quickly look at the sheet when they are writing. They can do this again and again. They can add new words and cross off words that they have learned. To get the message across even more, I ask students to make a copy and put it on their bedroom wall. So before they go to bed, while they are praying for another English teacher, they can quickly test themselves. It is all about familiarity and repetition. There are numerous ways to help students to remember certain words, but seeing them spelt correctly and knowing there is a sheet to consult helps to reinforce the correct form.

5. TIME AND DISTANCE

We want students to write with accuracy, but they often get the wrong view of writing. They assume, incorrectly, that accuracy just happens and that the quick two-second look they did will spot everything. Of course, we live in an age where people want things done quickly. We do want writing to be fluent by the end, but students need training for accuracy. A quick five minutes at the end of the work is not enough. Accuracy is improved by repeated reading.

Like most people, I make mistakes. I don't notice straightaway because I am too close. I often read what I think I have written and not what is actually there. And, annoyingly, the odd error slips through. Two words that always escape my brain when reading are 'think' and 'thing'. A quick read can well and truly confuse the reader. Students are like this too. They write in the moment. That's why they can write whole paragraphs without using full stops or whole stories without using paragraphs. To most, the ideas are more important than the style when you are in the flow of creativity. That is why handwriting can also be a problem. Students rush because they are worried that those really good ideas, like mice running around in their brain, are going to escape and disappear.

Build time in for students to forget what they have written. I don't think the next lesson is enough, to be honest. It needs to be at least a week. Coming to the text as a new reader gives them fresh eyes: students can then spot their own mistakes a mile off. They are quite happy to spot your typo on a PowerPoint or worksheet from ten paces with glee and pride. We are attuned to the errors of others. So many times I have been tempted to write to a publisher when I spot an error in a book. Of course, to speed things up you can get students to proofread each other's work; however, I think it is important that they each understand their mistakes.

Another solution is to get the students to read their work out loud. I often do this with my own writing and my wife thinks I have finally cracked under the pressures of work. Reading aloud helps, in my opinion, to break the link between what you think you have written and what you actually have. You see the mistakes and hear them glaringly. You look mad, of course, especially if you are reading a piece of creative writing and doing the various voices, but this is OK, good even.

6. VISIBILITY

A lot of students get the words 'a lot' wrong. In my time I have seen several versions, but the preferred option is usually 'allot' or 'alot'. Why is it that students make this mistake over and over again? Well, it is relatively simple. Say the following sentence out loud:

A lot of gardeners own or rent an allotment and the owner allots a fixed amount of space for each person.

Did you notice how you say 'a lot' in the same way as you say the opening of 'allotment' and 'allots'? You say it without any pauses. In fact, we all do it. Is there any wonder why students write it as one word when this is how it is spoken? To combat this, every time I come across it while reading aloud, I place emphasis on the gap and put a pause between the 'a' and the 'lot'. There are lots of mistakes students make and I think we have to be explicit about drawing attention to them.

7. HANDWRITING

At secondary school, handwriting becomes a bit of a mixed bag. There tends to be a clear divide between those who can and those who can't. And then you have the students who baffle you with their handwriting. The students who only write in capitals. The students who always put a love heart over the 'i'. The students who use capital letters wherever they want in a sentence or word or, bizarrely, only with words starting with the letter 'r'.

Handwriting is another way to judge students. Examiners might deny it, but there is a certain style that we expect from high-ability students. Either a variation of 'doctor's handwriting' or its opposite – perfection. Therefore, a student who has big, circular, bubbly handwriting that fills a line in four words gives the reader an impression that is probably unfavourable. I read it and see, regardless of gender, a student who day-dreams and has a pen that lights up when they write. I've had numerous arguments with students on this one because their handwriting is, to them, reflective of their 'individuality'. To which, I have responded: 'No, that's your haircut. Now, start writing like an adult.'

I am not going to tread down the path of 'cursive script' or 'not cursive script' but, instead, I am going to focus on making handwriting legible. Again, it is about the visual aspect of reading. Of course, we use phonics to break down unfamiliar words, but the majority of reading is based on word recognition and if the students are not using shapes that help readers to recognise the words, then they are going to struggle to convey their ideas.

A lot of the work I do with students is around the formation of letters and not the joining up of them. The first piece of writing with any class is my opportunity to set my stall out. I always focus on the handwriting and the presentation of the work. I will walk around the classroom monitoring the writing and advising students how to improve. Handwriting can be one of the biggest fixes and one of the quickest things to slip. Aside from students who struggle because of issues relating to fine motor skills, the majority of them can easily improve the presentation of their work. They just need a push. And some direct instruction.

My first lesson will address some of these issues:

- Writing that floats above the line.
- Writing that has capital letters the same size as the lower case letters.
- Writing that doesn't make the gaps between words obvious.
- Writing that is so big the letters fill the complete space between the lines on the paper.

I will highlight these issues in a student's work and ask them to address them. I might even model what I want to see. They say God or, occasionally, the Devil is in the detail. I think the details of handwriting should be addressed from the start. I have seen some of the biggest improvements in writing between the first and second lesson. We want to catch students making progress and reward them for those improvements, yet with writing that can be hard. By looking at handwriting from the beginning, I am able to spot improvements and changes and reward appropriately. If the attention to handwriting is there, it is likely that the attention to accuracy and content will be too.

Chapter 9
HOW TO TEACH GRAMMAR

Grammar has certainly been given a renewed lease of life thanks to recent changes in primary schools; students' knowledge has increased considerably and this can be an alarming thing as many, if not the majority of, teachers were not explicitly taught it themselves. The explicit teaching of grammar remains a contentious issue.

One of the arguments against is that the rules stifle creativity in students. This is the argument of many a children's author: writers who were taught the rules and have gone on to be successful by employing them or by deliberately going against them and calling it poetry. Rules are rules. Without rules we'd have chaos and disorder. There is a romantic notion that writing is purely spontaneous, lovely, fluffy and creative. Unless you are at the chalkboard, day in and day out, you can easily have the idea that writing is always wonderful, fun and exploratory. If I didn't have to worry about students passing exams and succeeding in life, I'd happily put away my planning and get them all to write ungrammatical epic fantasies to outdo *The Lord of the Rings*. But we are employed to make students better at our subject, and sometimes that involves learning and repeating the rules so that they don't break them when they are examined. Either that or teach them the rules so that they can be knowingly subversive by breaking them for effect. What the swathes of non-teachers who are against the explicit teaching of grammar don't get is that you can be creative and still follow the rules – indeed knowing them is a prerequisite to proper creativity. You can be ironic, sardonic and witty and follow the rules of grammar. Grammar forms the backbone of writing. It doesn't hinder creativity; it scaffolds it.

Over the years, I have seen lots of people start on the path to becoming a teacher. I worked with one who did everything on PowerPoint, including writing the date, and one who believed that the school rules didn't apply to him or his classes. The kids loved the latter, but not for the reasons he wanted them to. They loved the fact that they could chat all lesson, sit where they wanted and use their mobile phones. Within a term he discovered some boundaries. In fact, I believe he is now an assistant head with responsibility for ensuring the whole school, including the teaching staff, follow the rules. We need rules and boundaries for good reason. Without them, chaos ensues and nothing makes much sense. It takes an understanding of what happens when you don't follow the rules to know their value. Teachers are, by definition, generally clever people and, when looking at students' work, they try to make sense of what is written. They try to see past the imperfections. Sadly, life and examiners are not as optimistic or as understanding.

Accuracy with grammar means that written communication is clear, correct and unlikely to cause confusion with vagueness and uncertainty. We learn by making mistakes and if we don't talk about them, we are not improving. Talk about grammatical errors with colleagues. With students. With parents. Talk is the only thing that is going to address our collective fear, worry and anxiety relating to language use. We can't all be fortunate enough to have grammar guru David Crystal sat next to us, so we have to use the next best thing – us. Teachers will readily enthuse about how good a novel or poem is yet will refrain from mentioning the metalanguage behind its construction. A grammatical term remains just that – a term – unless we explore it.

Grammar is quite scientific and that's the beauty of it. A simile can be quite an abstract concept for students to grasp, but a preposition is concrete and functional – it is used to show where the subject is in relation to the object in the sentence or the relationship between (generally speaking) two nouns. Whereas with a simile, you could have billions of nuances and subtle shades of meaning. There's often a logical framework to grammar. Can what looks like a preposition be something else? Through some logical steps, we can work out if it is a preposition or not.[1] What looks like a simple preposition may in fact be an adverb, conjunction or preposition:

Is it followed by an object? A preposition.

Is it followed by a verb? Not a preposition.

Is it not followed by an object? An adverb.

Is it joining two clauses together? A conjunction.

---

1   For more guidance see: https://www.englishgrammar.org/conjunction-preposition/.

I have simplified the process, but there are exceptions to the rule. Yes, there are prepositions that don't need a noun, but then you go back to the rules again.

1. IN THE BEGINNING WAS THE NOUNS

There's quite a lot of terminology associated with language and, often, it is based on context. A word can be a verb in one sentence and an adjective in another. That's why we need a more thoughtful approach. It might be easy to list definitions for some things, but grammar needs scrutiny and thought before you chuck out an answer. We need thoughtful students and not ones who rush out terminology with little comprehension. We have all been there. We've identified a target in a sentence and asked a student to name the word class. There's panic in their eyes. They reel out a list with the hope of reaching jackpot eventually. 'Is it a verb ... a noun ... an adjective?'

When exploring word classes, I tend to take a very methodical approach. It goes: nouns, verbs, adjectives, adverbs, prepositions, conjunctions and so on. Nouns and verbs are the things students struggle less with, so that makes a good starting point. I'd use these questions to help with the identification:

Is it a word for a thing? Place? Person? It's a noun.

Is it an action, thought, process or state of being? It's a verb.

There is some confusion to be had with abstract nouns and the verbs 'to have' and 'to be', which should lead to a fruitful discussion with the class. In the following sentence, students usually have no problem spotting that 'teacher', 'cat' and 'mat' are all nouns and 'sat' is the verb.

The English teacher's cat sat lazily on the putrid and unclean mat.

Now students have the tent pegs of the sentence. Everything is held up by the verbs and nouns, so when you have these sorted, it is easier for them to spot the adjectives and adverbs, because they are related. I then get students to look at the use of adjectives – either by direct questioning or by simply asking students to pick out adjectives related to the nouns spotted.

What adjectives describe the mat? Putrid and unclean.

For me, the relationship between words is incredibly important. Yes, it might be great that a student can list a number of different adjectives, yet we will have difficulties if a student cannot explain that the writer used an adjective to describe a particular noun in a sentence. That is often the foundation for a lot of comprehension activities.

Once we have identified the adjectives, we go on to adverbs or prepositions.

What word describes how the cat sat? Lazily.

What word shows us where the cat is in relation to the mat? On.

We explore a sentence by focusing on nouns, verbs, adjectives and adverbs. Then the rest, if you want to be pedantic. This systematic approach is one students can adopt for all texts. But it does take time. You cannot rush grammar otherwise you get guesses. You can work on isolated word classes, such as spotting abstract and concrete nouns or different types of article; however, my best advice is to keep things focused on real texts. Lists help develop abstract notions of language. A concrete example is better and easier to grasp, from a student's point of view. When teaching grammar, we have to be careful we don't give students a warped view of language. It is perhaps easier to notice something when it is removed from context. However, the connectivity of words is missed when you isolate language features. This example could miss out the connection between 'lazily' and 'putrid and unclean'. There's a pattern of neglect and disinterest which the adjectives and adverb suggest. Each word connects to the next like dominos and that warrants exploration. How does one word modify our understanding of another? Why use 'the' English teacher instead of 'an' English teacher? What makes the 'English' teacher different to others? Why 'cat' and not 'dog'?

You could go on and on, exploring the tiny bits of meaning in just one sentence. Each word adds something. A slow exploration and looking at the links between words and meaning is far better than death by terminology.

2. TO CLAUSE OR NOT TO CLAUSE

Simple and compound sentences are pretty straightforward and easy to spot and discuss. When we get to complex sentences, things get a little vaguer in the minds of some students and their sentence construction can get pretty clunky. The building of a sentence is not just about adding words together, but about the position of them, their arrangement into clauses and the use of punctuation. There's more to think about with a complex sentence. They take more time, care and effort to teach.

I find that teaching clauses is incredibly useful when exploring texts and when students want to extend a sentence. However, it is often reduced to the simple use of specific words. Add 'although' to the end and write a bit more to make it a complex sentence. For me, teaching students how to use a subordinate clause is much more effective if the different parts are taught in isolation. Start with your weakest element first, then add your strongest. We know students can write main clauses because they have mastered simple and compound sentences from an early age, yet the majority struggle to use subordinate clauses effectively.

Typically, I start with a conditional clause – other types are available.

If I hadn't said something

I ask students, how could we turn this into a complete sentence? At this point, we might get into a healthy discussion about how the phrase on its own might be acceptable for speech and dialogue but not so for writing. It's important to highlight the differences between spoken and written modes – an area that students easily blur.

Then we get something like this:

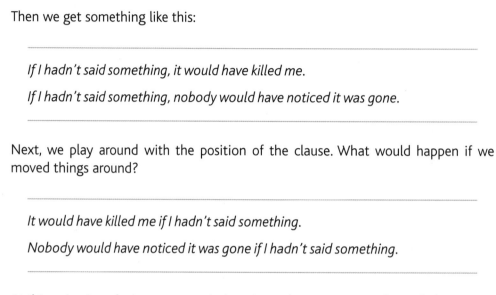

If I hadn't said something, it would have killed me.

If I hadn't said something, nobody would have noticed it was gone.

Next, we play around with the position of the clause. What would happen if we moved things around?

It would have killed me if I hadn't said something.

Nobody would have noticed it was gone if I hadn't said something.

At this point, it makes sense to remind students that a comma isn't needed in a complex sentence when the main clause is at the beginning.

The great thing is that students can then see how the subordinate clause works in relation to the main clause and how you can organise the sentence in different ways. The conditional clause offers a sense of mystery when positioned at the start; we get a sense of the person's thinking and that they put their thoughts and feelings first. Overall, this approach helps students to structure their thinking better. They have the ideas and understanding clauses helps them to communicate the ideas effectively.

3. SUBJECT/OBJECT

When discussing the subject of a sentence, we need to be clear with our students that the *subject* doesn't mean the *topic* of the sentence. By subject, we mean the person or thing that is doing the action (or having the action done unto them). Weak writers are often identified by their limited use of the subject, tending to repeat it and not offering alternative descriptions.

Looking at the subject of sentences is a good starting point for looking at texts. My personal approach is to identify the key verb and look for the noun linked to or 'doing' the verb.[2] Take this example from *The Sign of the Four* by Sir Arthur Conan Doyle.

> *Sherlock Holmes took his bottle from the corner of the mantel-piece and his hypo-dermic syringe from its neat morocco case. With his long, white, nervous fingers he adjusted the delicate needle, and rolled back his left shirt-cuff. For some little time his eyes rested thoughtfully upon the sinewy forearm and wrist all dotted and scarred with innumerable puncture-marks. Finally he thrust the sharp point home, pressed down the tiny piston, and sank back into the velvet-lined arm-chair with a long sigh of satisfaction.[3]*

It is vanishingly rare for students to make reference to the subject of a sentence, but there's always something interesting to say about the writer's use of the subject and how it varies from sentence to sentence. For example, Conan Doyle starts with the proper noun 'Sherlock Holmes' and two of the succeeding sentences maintain the subject but replace the name with the pronoun 'he'. What is interesting is that the third sentence changes the subject from 'Sherlock Holmes' to 'his eyes': it narrows the focus. This possibly gives the idea that Holmes is hesitant. This subtle change isn't always noticeable, especially when you look at the previous sentence and see how the writer describes 'his long, white, nervous fingers', which, on first viewing, could easily be mistaken for the subject of that sentence. Students should look for the changes in subject and discuss why it is placed where it is.

---

2   If you are struggling, I'd recommend a parsing website. See http://www.link.cs.cmu.edu/link/submit-sentence-4.html, for example.

3   A. Conan Doyle, *The Sign of the Four* (Project Gutenberg ebook edition, 2008 [1890]), ch 1. Available at: http://www.gutenberg.org/files/2097/2097-h/2097-h.htm.

Then we look at the next paragraph:

> *Three times a day for many months I had witnessed this performance, but custom had not reconciled my mind to it. On the contrary, from day to day I had become more irritable at the sight, and my conscience swelled nightly within me at the thought that I had lacked the courage to protest. Again and again I had registered a vow that I should deliver my soul upon the subject, but there was that in the cool, nonchalant air of my companion which made him the last man with whom one would care to take anything approaching to a liberty. His great powers, his masterly manner, and the experience which I had had of his many extraordinary qualities, all made me diffident and backward in crossing him.*[4]

The focus moves as the subject changes to the first person and that first person is Doctor Watson – the story is told from his perspective.

Of course, we can extend the focus and include objects. However, I feel that the subject is a good starting point and one we can easily access and approach. At the same time, we can look at the writing. As we see how Conan Doyle varies the subject of his sentences, we are modelling how our students might do this and weave cohesion across a paragraph in their own writing.

One thing I do when exploring the subject is to get students writing using the structure the writer has employed. You can easily model it for them:

Sherlock Holmes

He

His eyes

He

And it works for non-fiction too. More often than not, the subjects are more interesting in non-fiction and more integral to getting the writer's ideas across.

---

4   Conan Doyle, *The Sign of the Four*, ch 1.

4. NOUN PHRASES AND VERB PHRASES

Somewhere in the dark ooze at the bottom of the Thames lie the bones of that strange visitor to our shores.[5]

Noun phrases and verb phrases are especially important in literary texts because they add meaning and nuance. They also help students to develop writing without the need to add ten extra conjunctions. In the above sentence we can see the following noun phrases:

the dark <u>ooze</u>

the bottom of the <u>Thames</u>

the <u>bones</u> of that strange visitor to our shores

Noun phrases also help to make students more precise in their writing. They will often chuck nouns at the reader, but only the more skilled will add the precise detail and expand them into noun phrases. Getting students to see how and why a writer has developed a noun phrase is really quite useful.

Knowledge of noun phrases and verb phrases is something we need to work harder on in the classroom. We need to be reading texts to experience and comment on them so, in turn, students can absorb, learn and recall them for later use.

I get them to learn these structures:

- adjective noun
- adjective, adjective noun
- adjective, adjective and adjective noun
- adjective, adjective, adjective noun
- adjective and adjective noun

---

5   Conan Doyle, *The Sign of the Four*, ch 10.

If students learn the syntax of noun phrases, their memory is focused on this rather than the 'I must remember to use adjectives' approach. There's so much going on in our heads when we write that it helps to have preformed syntactical structures to hand. Students then are drilled on the above so that they know that whenever they need to describe a noun they have several options for doing so.

5. MODELLING SENTENCES

The danger with teaching grammar is in its decontextualisation into a single unit. In reality, every lesson is an opportunity to model and explore sentence structure. You'll recall Alan Peat's approach – inventing names for certain sentence structures. For example:

'The more ... the more ...'

The more I read, the more I feel that the world is a wonderful and rich place.

Naming and identifying structures of writing helps students to recreate sentences and build their own. But it also has merit in exploring grammar. In a way, students create their own language for structuring language. Yes, we could talk about simple, complex and compound sentences, but they can be less than useful when analysing structure. Using terminology like 'prepositional phrase' or 'relative phrase' helps more.

Let's go back to *The Sign of the Four* by Conan Doyle.

We were fairly after her now. The furnaces roared, and the powerful engines whizzed and clanked, like a great metallic heart. Her sharp, steep prow cut through the river-water and sent two rolling waves to right and to left of us. With every throb of the engines we sprang and quivered like a living thing. One great yellow lantern in our bows threw a long, flickering funnel of light in front of us. Right ahead a dark blur upon the water showed where the Aurora lay, and the swirl of white foam behind her spoke of the pace at which she was going. We flashed past barges, steamers, merchant-vessels, in and out, behind this one and round the other.

Voices hailed us out of the darkness, but still the Aurora thundered on, and still we followed close upon her track.[6]

How would students describe some of the sentences in this passage? How would they name them?

The furnaces roared, and the powerful engines whizzed and clanked, like a great metallic heart.

Student: It's a 'three sounds and a simile' sentence.

We flashed past barges, steamers, merchant-vessels, in and out, behind this one and round the other.

Student: It's a 'list of things followed by their positions' sentence.

The great thing is that at this stage students have a model to work with and they can create their own versions.

The cars screeched, screamed and bellowed, like an angry child.

I walked past men, women and children, behind, near, next to me.

When students have studied the sentence and explored the structure, it becomes easier for us, as teachers, to bridge the gap between the student's language and the metalanguage we want. It's quite an exploratory method, but it allows us to teach grammar terminology and let the students take the lead, at least in part.

The furnaces roared, and the powerful engines whizzed and clanked, like a great metallic heart.

Student: It's a 'three sounds and a simile' sentence.

---

6   Conan Doyle, *The Sign of the Four*, ch 10.

Teacher: The sentence has a parenthetical clause and this, by definition, makes it a complex sentence. What happens to the sentence if you remove the clause?

We flashed past barges, steamers, merchant-vessels, in and out, behind this one and round the other.

Student: It's a 'list of things of followed by their positions' sentence.

Teacher: This is a simple sentence followed by three prepositional phrases.

The teacher can then extend and develop the student's grammatical knowledge and understanding of the text.

When students explore the grammar of a text, they are likely to get it wrong and right. It is just that they usually don't get it right enough. This approach allows students to explore and work out the puzzle of the sentence for themselves. The teacher doesn't comment on whether the student is right or wrong, but further explores the underlying grammar, helping them understand the rules of a particular sentence. They are articulating the structure and grammar of the sentence in a safe way, allowing students more opportunities to offer ideas and a greater chance of getting it correct.

6. PURPOSE AND EFFECT

There's a lot of time spent working on the knowledge of a specific grammatical term, its definition and the ability to identify an example in a text. We teach students what a noun, conjunction and complex sentence is and how to spot one, yet we often neglect emotional impact of each one. By simply using a specific word or sentence we can change the mood, purpose and impact of the text. Students don't just need basic grammar knowledge, but they need contextual knowledge for grammar use, as language is always dependent on the context in which it is being used.

Take this question: how could you avoid putting the blame on a person when writing?

A violent student viciously punched a teacher last week in a small, friendly secondary school.

What could students do?

- Remove the adjectives.
- Remove the adverbs.
- Use the passive voice.

You could end up with the following sentence:

A teacher was punched in a secondary school.

Comparing the two sentences shows you the effect of each of the grammatical aspects. And it can be taken further when you add another comparative sentence.

A teacher was punched in a secondary school.

An individual was attacked in a school.

The second sentence now has a degree of ambiguity that might cause fear in a parent because the sentence now refers to any school and anybody in one. Placing the emphasis on the impact and effect of these choices shows students how to use grammatical devices. Sadly, the teaching of writing has become affected too much by increased levels of accountability and a focus on exam performance and outcomes. This, in turn, has created a type of alien writing, concerned only with 'bolted-on' aspects rather than making a text fit its purpose and audience. Students will, therefore, choose a device for the examiner rather than select it because it is the most effective way of communicating something in that context.

We need to work on providing students with a range of different contexts for using language and show them how language varies from context to context. We need to embrace the richness of language and avoid the narrowness of a clear list of features to use in a specific, narrow and unrealistic context.

7. FUSE WRITING AND READING

Every text studied in the classroom presents an opportunity for a discussion of grammar. It is just a shame that we place a greater, rather than equal, emphasis on meaning and literary devices. Often the slant of poetry analysis is on the use of literary devices. Or a specific word choice. Let's look at a poem from a grammatical perspective.

Ozymandias

I met a traveller from an antique land

Who said: Two vast and trunkless legs of stone

Stand in the desert ... Near them, on the sand,

Half sunk, a shattered visage lies, whose frown,

And wrinkled lip, and sneer of cold command,

Tell that its sculptor well those passions read

Which yet survive, stamped on these lifeless things,

The hand that mocked them and the heart that fed:

And on the pedestal these words appear:

'My name is Ozymandias, king of kings:

Look on my works, ye Mighty, and despair!'

Nothing beside remains. Round the decay

Of that colossal wreck, boundless and bare

The lone and level sands stretch far away.[7]

From a grammatical point of view, this is quite a rich text. How would we use our knowledge to unlock it?

- The first sentence is a simple sentence with a relative clause – 'who'.

- There are numerous examples of noun phrases – 'vast and trunkless legs'/ 'shattered visage'

- The last sentence starts with a prepositional phrase – 'Round the decay'.

- The subject varies from the narrator ('I') to the statue ('legs of stone') to its face ('a shattered visage') to nothing ('Nothing beside remains') to the desert ('lone and level sands').

In fact, I'd say that if a student has a good understanding of the choices made by Shelley, then they have a better understanding of the poem than if they can simply regurgitate the knowledge that it is a sonnet. Why? Well, because the grammar points are really structural points. Picking up on a grammatical aspect is examining the skeleton of a text whereas spotting a literary device is only picking at the skin.

- Understand the use of relative clauses and you understand the emphasis on what is left and what is lost.

- Understand the use of noun phrases and you understand the physical nature of all that has been lost.

- Understand the use of the conjunction to start a sentence and you understand that the pedestal is the most important thing left as it identifies who the person was.

Any text should be read with 'grammar goggles'. Students lose their grammatical knowledge if it isn't explored and talked about repeatedly. And students love rules.

---

7   P. B. Shelley, 'Ozymandias', in T. Hutchinson (ed.), *The Complete Poetical Works of Percy Bysshe Shelley Volume II* (Project Gutenberg ebook edition, 2003 [Oxford: Oxford University Press, 1914, poem first published 1818]). Available at: http://www.gutenberg.org/cache/epub/4798/pg4798-images.html.

Publicly they won't admit it, but they like a structure to follow. Change the structure of a lesson and students don't like it. We have a subconscious need for patterns and repetition. Music is repeated patterns. Poetry is repeated patterns. Genres and stories are repeating the same pattern and changing the names. We have morning and evening routines. They get things done. Repeat. Repeat.

Grammar is about patterns too. However, we need to teach students the patterns and work with them regularly so that they become habitualised. Take the use of capital letters. Capitals should be used for proper nouns and at the start of a sentence, and students need to automate their knowledge of these patterns. When they have internalised that pattern, they don't make too many mistakes with it. Our job is to help them to subsume the more complex patterns of language, and the starting point is for the teacher to be explicit about their existence.

Chapter 10
HOW TO TEACH WRITING
– PART 2

Writing is so important that the seven simple ideas covered in Part 1 will never be anywhere near enough to cover the difficulties inherent in getting students to write well. I'd love to say that writing in my classroom is like something out of *Mary Poppins*: I simply sing a jaunty educational tune and the students write with glee and joy as I twirl about. Sadly, and rather more prosaically, my classroom environment is more akin to a Roman ship with me beating a metaphorical drum at the back. Boom. Boom. Boom. Write, you dogs!

How do we get all students writing to the beat of the drum? Well, I think we need to form clear patterns and processes for writing. We need to signal when the lesson is a writing lesson. How you do that in your classroom is up to you. Students need to be clear what a 'heads down and write' lesson looks like. And we need to repeat that process and train students so that they get used to it. The problems happen when you haven't signalled that it is a writing lesson. Writing, for most people, involves having a silent working environment. Silence is important as it helps channel thought and focuses our attention on the paper and the job. In drama, you have the idea of the 'suspension of disbelief' and this is a state that playgoers experience in a theatre. There is an equivalent in writing. Let's call it the 'suspension of artifice'. Students know that what they are doing is fake. They know that the head teacher isn't going to change their opinion on the school's uniform based on their well-formed argument. They know that the BBC isn't going to take on board their suggestions about what might make *EastEnders* less unrealistic. They know that the Queen isn't going to read the letter persuading her to knight their English teacher. But that teacher needs to create the artificial bubble of context so students write with an audience in mind. The writing is real, but the context isn't. And just as actors and stage crew work hard to create the suspension of disbelief by ensuring silence except for the actors on stage and that all is in darkness apart from the stage, teachers need to work on creating the same environment. Theatre audiences buy into and support the rules. Set the rules and place the focus on the stage and its actors.

As with actors, there are various types of writer. There's the hesitant writer who doubts their ability. There's the writer who throws everything at the reader. There's the writer who is perceptive and insightful with every word and sentence. There's the writer who will not even start until their demands are met. I have seen them all. The context for writing is a challenging one in any classroom. We are asking students to make their thoughts concrete. We are asking them to produce something visible and readable. Something that can be judged. We are, in some ways, asking them to bare their soul. I have seen the most articulate students crumble under the portentousness of picking up their pen. We aren't so critical of verbal contributions and of speech in general, but with writing we (and I mean society here) can be prone to being hypercritical. We know it has to be perfect. Students know it has to be perfect and that worries them. Writing well is perceived to be the single most important and universal marker of intelligence in education.

The desire for perfection in writing has become a real problem for English teaching. We know that students will make mistakes and our job is to help them eventually stop doing so, but a lot of students' hesitancy is related to our view of what constitutes useful writing. Students see endless examples of 'perfect' writing. Many lessons are given over to reading work by the greats. We give model examples. Of themselves, these are fine, but subconsciously we are feeding the view that only perfection is acceptable. There is no in-between state. Perfect or not perfect. What if you are that student who knows their work is very far from perfect? The students who are close to perfection are usually well-motivated because they are a pen stroke away from genuinely useful competence, but the students who are a fair way from that state know it because they have perfection paraded before them every lesson. This creates boundaries and mental blocks. Why bother if you know you are opening yourself up to criticism? A lot of my time is spent with these students. I am trying to undo the behaviours they have adopted given our conditioning, trying to divest them of the layers of protection that I, myself, have caused them to don.

Writing isn't as simple as it seems. It is emotionally, physically and psychologically complex. We need to work out the thinking behind unproductive behaviours in writing. Have a think about these examples. What do you think is the real issue at play with these students?

1   The student who writes absolute rubbish but is always the first to finish the task.

2   The bright student who spends ages on a single paragraph.

3   The articulate student who writes pages and pages without using any punctuation at all.

4   The naughty student who produces dull writing, but always writes enough.

I have taught many students like this over the years and some of my solutions to dealing with the problem are as follows:

1   The student who writes absolute rubbish but is always the first to finish the task.

    This student hasn't had much success with their work, but the one thing they can do is complete it first. They crave positive encouragement from finishing first, so they work hard to ensure they get it.

    Solution: Get the student to lead the whole class in writing a response. They become the one who controls how others work. The class finish when they have finished. The speed at which they write affects the rest of the class. Students have to match the pace of this one student. What happens when you do this is that the student becomes aware of how others write at a different pace. All I need to do is shout out to the student, 'What paragraph are you on now?' The class have to match the dominant writer. Another strategy is to get the student to work with a partner. However, the partner is the writer and the student in question gives ideas and suggestions. This adds an extra level of thought to the writing which is often lacking in the student's work.

2   The bright student who spends ages on a single paragraph.

    This student is searching for perfection. They are trying to control all aspects of the writing. They might actually lack confidence and doubt their own ability. They are hypercritical of their own work to the point that they can't move on. Often, these students have a tainted view of perfection. They often create excellent pieces of work, but they are in the 'eye of the storm' so lack self-awareness.

Solution: Give the student clear time limits for the writing. Do this as a whole class thing or as an individual 'intervention' if you want to be fancy. Give the students an eight minute block to work on a paragraph. Once the time is up, they move on. I find it also helps to have something physically blocking the writing. A pencil case works for this. As soon as a paragraph is completed, the pencil case covers the offending work. Another strategy is to give them an example or style model to work with. Allow them to have a point of comparison as their perspective is currently a bit warped. They feel the need to have fifteen similes and twelve rhetorical questions. The example gives them a visual reminder that you don't need to use every technique under the sun to be effective.

3   The articulate student who writes pages and pages without using any punctuation at all.

This type of student is quite common. Rarely have I come across a student who can't use some form of punctuation. Often, they have a case of more ideas than tools to express them. This student's keenness shouldn't be quashed. They just need the physical tools to ensure that their thought process is smoothed and channelled. At the moment, like a broken tap, everything is gushing out at once.

Solution: I like to get students to pair up and do a little bit of transcribing work. One student talks through their ideas for the task while the other writes. They take turns, then they have a rough plan and a starting position for the writing. They have a draft to work on and can add punctuation. Another strategy is to refuse to mark work until you have seen proof that they have addressed this. All too often, students write and don't give it a second look. They treat it like speech and that *doesn't* need retrospective self-regulation and revision. As I have explained, if we accept the work and correct the punctuation ourselves, we are giving them the message that this is OK. You only have to refuse to mark work once or twice for the student to make a change. I will admit it is quite a shock, but it draws a line in the sand.

4   The naughty student who produces dull writing, but always writes enough.

This student is an interesting one because they highlight a problem that I think is quite prevalent in most schools: 'phoning in' a performance. This student has developed a style of written waffling which they use in most subjects. This is very much how I wrote when I was at school. I could waffle for England. The teacher would give me a task and I would happily write stuff. It was bland and beige, but it kept the teacher off my back and it lightly addressed the task. A lot of boys use this approach; it is easy to do and doesn't take much thought or effort.

Solution: Describe and identify this as 'phoned in' writing. Make students aware of it. Often students are unaware of what they are doing because it is such a common practice for them. I spend time looking at writing in lessons. With one group, 'phoned in' writing was easily characterised by the use of 'because', 'and therefore' and 'furthermore'. Students would scroll through these in their non-fiction writing. They'd rotate through these words to address the task, but they'd simply be listing ideas with the odd bit of reasoning thrown in. I forbid these words and added that they could only begin one sentence in each paragraph with the word 'the', 'it' or 'this'.

Another strategy is to be brutal with redrafting. We can be a little bit too positive when giving feedback. We focus on what went well and what will make fast improvements. I think there are times, and it's up to the teacher to decide, when a red pen needs to be used to draw lines through whole sections of perfunctory text. Telling the student a sentence is meaningless is far more constructive than pleasantries and vagueness. I will tell students when a sentence is pointless and when a sentence is repeating an idea. Clear and constructive criticism is needed when we want students to make improvements. Tough love is required and smothering students in a blanket of kindness will only take them to a certain point. Watch a PE teacher and you'll see that relentless and determined pushing; they will pick up on when a student is capable of performing better and cajole them to do so. We lack that in the English classroom at times. We need to get better at telling them when things are 'crap'. But maybe don't use that word.

The eyes are said to be the windows to the soul. I'd say writing is the front door. In my classroom, there are thirty different reasons why students write the way they do.

That might range from the student who writes really small so I can't read their words and judge them, or the student who writes so big that it seems (and fails) to mask the fact that they haven't written much at all. Every student is different and each has a reason to behave as they do. It is too easy to blame issues with writing on their ability, their primary school or their previous English teacher. Writing is emotional and, while I am not suggesting that you have weekly therapy sessions with students as they write, I am suggesting that, before we look for an easy excuse or a 'get-out clause', we explore the student's emotional connection to writing. If writing is the front door to the soul, and that door is locked shut, there's probably a reason why. It is our job to talk to them to find out what it is and what we can do.

1. GETTING IN 'THE ZONE'

I know nothing about cars, but I always refer to them when explaining the writing process. Students like to think that they are Ferraris with the ability to go from 0 to 200 miles per hour in five seconds (this is my estimation – I told you I don't know much about cars) when, in reality, they are more Ford Fiesta and take that bit longer to get up to speed. The gap between thought and writing is one we need to actively work on. You can't go from nought to Jane Austen in five seconds. We need to get students to see the gap between thought and writing. Unlike speech, writing is not spontaneous – well, it shouldn't be. We need to challenge this. Yes, for the exams writing will need to seem spontaneous in creation, but it doesn't need to be during the four-and-a-half years spent preparing.

How do we get students into 'the zone' for writing? I think the first five minutes and the reveal of a task is important.

Today, I want you to write me a description of a classroom. I am looking for 300 words. You have a picture for inspiration.

When I am looking at your work, I want to see that you have used repetition, noun phrases and some original word choices.

I want you to make it really interesting for me and to show off. Do something original.

Are there any questions?

I always have the task on a PowerPoint slide so that students have an aide-memoire. But the set-up is an important stage and one we can easily neglect. We want independence with writing, but that comes from familiarity with the process, so we need to normalise it. The questions I get in response are always interesting. Take these examples:

1   Does it matter what colour pen I use?

2   Can I use something I have written in my book already?

3   Do I have to use the picture?

4   What is a noun phrase again?

It is during this questioning stage that you can address the issues and stop further mistakes from occurring. We want students to make the right kind of mistakes. I feel this level of questioning helps prevent more obvious ones. Question 1 shows a lack of common sense and knowledge of the basic classroom expectations. Students should be able to answer that one themselves. I often refuse to answer, asking the students to provide me with a possible answer. Question 4 is a knowledge question but an important one. I'd always ask the class to ensure all students know it and simply to revise the concept.

Questions 2 and 3 are interesting because, as first glance, they seem simple but, fundamentally, they relate to aspects that could constrict and hinder progress. If the student feels that they can't use something they have already written, they are going to have to think of something new and that could take time. If the student feels that they 'have to' use the picture then their work is possibly going to be limited.

Once I have gone through the questions, I give students five minutes to talk and prepare. This allows them to articulate ideas or thoughts. Usually, I'd get them to write these down in note form. Planning and idea forming don't need silence, but writing does. Finally, I ask if there are any more questions. Then I get students to write. During this, I will walk around the class reading their work. At this point, I might focus on students who I know may struggle and reassure them. I might tick a word or a phrase I like in order to motivate them. I repeat this process again and again. I will only interrupt the task if students are all getting the same thing wrong. I have witnessed some teachers give a constant commentary during a writing lesson: 'Don't forget to …', 'Remember you might want …', 'I don't do …' The process needs silence and the teacher has to lead by example.

2. OPENING/CLOSING SENTENCES

'How do I start it, sir?' This question is asked so often, it's as if all their problems lie within the opening sentence. Give them one and this is magically cured. This is a strategy I like to use again and again with students. I show them these openings to a task about persuading people to not smoke:

1   Cough. Cough. Sorry, I am struggling to say this as – cough, cough – I find it difficult to talk as I have had one lung removed due to cancer.

2   Smoking is bad. It is the cause of millions of deaths every year.

3   I know you can't help it, but smoking is terrible and it makes you stink.

4   £2,500 is exactly how much money you waste on smoking each year.

5   I am going to teach you about the dangers of smoking. In this article, I will give you the reasons as to why you shouldn't smoke.

6   Imagine you are on a date. Your date arrives. In the distance, they look gorgeous and worth the hours it has taken you to get ready. As they get closer, you notice something – a smell. The scent of an ashtray.

I am going to go back to my point about putting ideas first when writing. All too often students don't put much thought into that first sentence. Just as they begin a pretty substandard letter, they default to explaining what they are doing.

In this letter, I am writing to complain about the school uniform.

Yawn! A rudimentary start that will be followed by more rudimentary thinking wrapped up in rudimentary paragraphs. The clichéd or predictable approach is the easiest one to replicate. That's why we get stories ending with a dream or simplistic storytelling from the start. Students write their own rules at times. Teachers must actively work against clichés, student-formed rules and basic approaches to writing. By the time students are in Years 5 to 7, they should have been exposed to lots of different texts and have learned the basics of each genre. That's why we need to work hard to combat clichéd writing. It is easier for students, but it lacks subtlety and thought. Take this example:

In the year 2136, the double-headed people of Zarg-7 didn't like strangers and so, when the spaceship landed on the landing, both sets of eyes were staring at it.

This sentence appears to contain some technical skill, but is lacking in creativity. Writers will rarely signal a time period so obviously. Instead, they hint at the date in a way that appears more natural. The fact that the story is set in the future is important, but it doesn't have to be the first thing mentioned. You can point towards the idea with hints and clues instead of great signposts and massive posters. Teaching students to write is about subtlety, digression and breaking their own rules. The move from explicit to implicit thinking doesn't just apply to reading in secondary schools; it applies to writing. We need to help students develop the implicit.

Starting with the purpose of the writing is what explicit writers do. 'I am writing this letter to inform you I want the job.' The key question is: does it need explaining that the text is a letter? You don't need to give away your intent from the start. The best writers don't spell everything out. The best letters often get to the intent in paragraph two or three. This allows the writer to build a connection with the reader. Take the examples below:

Dear Mr Smith,

I have admired your work for a long time and I think your charitable efforts need recognition.

Dear Mr Smith,

In this letter, I am writing to complain about the school uniform.

Which opening is better? The first is because it starts to build a relationship with the reader. It shows what the writer thinks of them with the word 'admired' and it uses a positive and warm tone. It is better because it implies a lot more than the second one does, such as how the head teacher seems like a nice person because of his charity work, and so might be more responsive to requests. Implicit writing focuses more on feelings, mood, atmosphere, relationships and particular effects. We need to help students move towards the most meaningful approach in a given context.

Unlocking the potential of an opening sentence is important, and this is where I think teachers need to be careful with sentence starters as students merely copy and absorb these ideas. I think it is better to model examples rather than provide crutches. I often take the six sentences about smoking and use them to approach a piece of non-fiction. But, and here's the important thing, I make sure that the task is thematically removed from the examples used. Otherwise, we end up with mirror copies. Students can use the ideas or the style, but they can't copy the sentences.

I feel that having a bank of opening sentences is much better because you are getting students to see the endless possibility in the choices they could make; you are also showing them how their preconceived rules about writing might be challenged. Often they struggle to start because they are not used to writing in a particular style and, as a result, they gravitate towards clichés. However, by secondary school they should be confident with writing in various styles and just need a metaphorical kick to focus their little grey cells. I do the same with conclusions too:

---

1   So, if you want to be another statistic on a long and ever expanding list, then carry on smoking.

2   Finally, the reasons for not smoking are clear – it is bad; it causes cancer; it stunts your growth; it costs a lot of money.

3   Act now and stub it out or expect to be ash quicker than you think.

4   Smoking costs. Smoking smells. Smoking kills.

5   To conclude, smoking is very bad; so, to save your life, do something now.

Modelling can take several guises and this is just one. Instead of placing a piece of perfection in front of a student, give them several options. Get them to work out what makes good work good. Also, give students permission to experiment with writing. Unless they see that it is acceptable to start with a lyric from a song, they will more often than not refrain from doing so. Giving them different examples allows them to write their own rules. I can use repetition. I can use humour. I can use anecdote. Modelling helps to rewire the brain and overwrite the 'rules' that students have composed over the years.

3. SETTING AND THE BASIC BUILDING BLOCKS FOR CREATING MEANING

There is an elephant in the room when we talk about teaching writing, and that is the students' lack of experience. They have little experience of how writers structure and order things, so they struggle to accommodate these concepts. There's no real surprise that the best writers in a class are often the regular readers. It is as if with every book they read they pick up one little nugget of gold. The more they read, the more nuggets you are likely to spot in their work.

The difficult question for any teacher is how to bridge the gap between inexperience and its more grown up cousin. We want inexperienced readers to write like experienced readers. What can we do to support this? Again, I'd say we need to be explicit about the choices students can make and their impact. Let's take setting. Describing a setting is one of the writing tasks in the new GCSE and, to be honest, most stories feature some description, otherwise they would take place in an empty void. But how the setting is described has an incredibly important effect and meaning.

I give students the following list of choices a writer might make when describing a location. I get them to pick four. From the start, I'll always make it clear what sort of effect the writing needs to create.

Describe a sound and then reveal what is causing it.

Describe normality and then spot something that isn't normal.

Describe something that isn't really there and is just imagined by the narrator.

Describe the feeling of the place. Don't describe anything else, just the feeling. *It feels like a day ... It feels like when a ...*

Describe an object but make it sound like something else. Then reveal what it really is.

Describe the movement of an object or part of the object. Give a list of verbs describing the action.

Something is blocking your view of the object. Describe what's blocking your view and describe the tiny glimpse you get of the object you want to see.

Describe how an object's appearance changes the closer you get to it.

Describe the lack of something. *There isn't a ... or a ... or a ...*

Describe the texture of an object before revealing what it is.

Describe a nice object and then an unpleasant object.

Describe a change in the room.

Describe the main source of light and how it touches things in the setting.

Describe a moment of silence.

Describe an object and then comment on how it links to/reflects the owner of the room.

Describe a change in temperature and the narrator's exploration of the source of the change.

Describe the light and how it falls. Then describe it falling on an object.

Describe an object through colours. Then reveal what it is.

Describe three objects using the same phrase.

Describe an object as if it were a person.

Describe how an object links, or doesn't link, to another item next to it.

Describe how an object reminds the narrator of something that happened to them.

Describe how an object reminds the narrator of a similar object from their past.

Imagine I'm a student writing about a setting that was peaceful. I might select the following choices:

Describe the main source of light and how it touches things in the setting.

Describe a moment of silence.

Describe a sound and then reveal what is causing it.

Describe the light and how it falls. Then describe it falling on an object.

Let's say I'm describing a classroom and trying to make that sound peaceful. Oh the irony. I might come up with sentences like these:

Tables, chairs and displays felt the warm glow of the light gently stretched across them.

Time stopped still. It breathed in and held its breath. Silence.

The rhythm of soft, scratching noise could be heard again and again as the clock watched on.

Sunlight from the window blanketed itself across everything.

Then, when I have these ready, I can play around with the structure of the paragraph and add extra sentences if needed.

Sunlight from the window blanketed itself across everything. Tables, chairs and displays felt the warm glow of the light gently stretched across them. The rhythm of soft, scratching noise could be heard again and again as the clock watched on. Time stopped still. It breathed in and held its breath. Silence.

The transformation from the original list to the final paragraph has involved several choices. I started with light to help focus on the atmosphere. I felt that the silence should go after the ticking of the clock as it made the ending of the paragraph more dramatic. What we have here is a structured piece of writing that has been created with very little teacher input. The beauty of this approach is that you are teaching students to see the choices in their own writing, and this will inform their analysis of the work of other writers.

I typically follow this activity by reading a description by another writer. Of course, there are hundreds of possibilities and my list is not definitive, but it gives students an idea of how writers have options. They could see how Dickens uses two of these, partly, in a description in *Great Expectations*:

> *This was very uncomfortable, and I was half afraid. However, the only thing to be done being to knock at the door, I knocked and was told from within to enter. I entered, therefore, and found myself in a pretty large room that was well lighted with wax candles. No glimpse of daylight was to be seen in it. It was a dressing-room, as I supposed from the furniture, though much of it was of forms and uses then quite unknown to me. But prominent in it was a draped table with a gilded looking-glass, and that I made out at first sight to be a fine lady's dressing-table.*[1]

They could go even further and articulate how the writer structured the extract and create their own descriptions, if necessary.

- Describe the narrator's feelings.

- Describe a sound.

- Describe the source of the light.

- Describe the lack of other sources of light.

- Describe what the light has fallen onto.

- Describe an object with the most light on it.

Then we can explore the reasons behind Dickens' choice. What is the impact of starting with the narrator's feelings? Why focus on sound rather than light first?

Reading is the performance-enhancing drug that all students need in English. Even if we cram every lesson with reading, more is always needed to become highly proficient. Sometimes, we need a purer form of the drug. We need to give them the insight that is only gained naturally from a reading habit. This is the closest we can get to making students voracious readers without sitting with them every day listening to them read. It is about making the implicit explicit to the students.

---

1   Dickens, *Great Expectations*, ch 8.

4. REPETITION

Deliberate repetition is one of the most underused techniques, and it is one of the easiest to deploy in any piece of writing. If a student has a limited vocabulary, it can be hard to tell them to use better words, but anyone can use repetition for effect provided you have given them explicit permission to do so. Students tend to think that repetition means lazy and boring writing. How many times do we moan when things are repetitive and monotonous? It is understandable when a student is writing and hoping to achieve 'perfection' that they want to avoid something with usually negative association.

When getting students to write a creative piece, I always show them how repetition can be used for effect. I like to do this with a before and after.

Example 1: *The water trickled down the walls as I walked through the cave. Silence. I felt uncertain about what to do. My eyes started to get used to the lack of light. Then. I saw it.*

I often get students to have a go at adding repetition to the example before showing one I've prepared earlier. Either that or I amend the example on the visualiser.

Example 2: *The water tricked down the walls, down the stalagmites, down the stalactites, as I walked through the cave. Silence. I felt uncertain about what to do, uncertain what to think, uncertain what to wonder. Silence. My eyes started to get used to the lack of light. Silence. My eyes focused. My eyes saw something. Far. Close. Near. By me.*

We discuss the benefits of repeating things in the pattern of three and how that plays with our expectations in a story. Then I get students to explore how paragraphing can be used for effect.

Example 3: *The water tricked down the walls, down the stalagmites, down the stalactites, as I walked through the cave.*

Silence.

I felt uncertain about what to do, uncertain what to think, uncertain what to wonder.

Silence.

My eyes started to get used to the lack of light.

Silence. My eyes focused. My eyes saw something.

Far.

Close.

Near.

By me.

I find that when you give students the permission to use repetition you get some of their best writing. And I make it the focus for a piece of work. I make sure I'm not asking them to use seventeen different techniques at the same time. I want them to use repetition for effect. But we have to challenge the notion that repetition is boring. I said, repetition is not boring. Not boring at all.

5. TALK ABOUT CLICHÉD WRITING

We need to talk about clichéd writing regularly in lessons. We need to be explicit with students about what is clichéd and what isn't. Added to that, we need to explain when and why writing sounds childish. We'd all like students to produce original and creative writing, and we'll show examples that typify that kind of work; however, we rarely call a spade a spade when discussing writing. We protect students from it. We'll spot the accuracy errors and highlight the really good bits, but we rarely highlight the boring, the predictable or the clichéd. Take this example:

The car zoomed down the street like a bullet. Crash!

There comes a point in writing when the use of onomatopoeia is childish. It isn't something good writers generally use – and if they do, it is done subtly. Then there is the simile 'like a bullet'. It's vastly too predictable. It is shorthand in a way. The student has some readily recalled phrases in their head and they use them to get 'their' ideas down quickly. With just a little bit of thought, that writing could be easily transformed.

The car swerved and skidded like a criminal's polygraph test.

You'll notice that 'zoomed' has changed to 'swerved and skidded' and that's because, sometimes, the words in the rest of the sentence present the writer with no other choice but to use cliché when writing a simile. 'Zoomed' is probably one of those verbs to which there are only four similes left in the universe that we could apply without sounding like a cliché. Curse all those primary school children writing poems about rockets and fireworks; they have singlehandedly drained that verb of any creative simile potential.

The danger is that there are clichés everywhere in English and some clichés are possibly more palatable than others. Ideally, we want students to select the more uncommon ones or create their own original phrases. However, we need to show the gradients in predictable writing, and we need to call it out when the most obvious ones have been used. Try ranking the following in terms of how clichéd they are:

1   *The car swerved and skidded like a supermarket trolley with a mind of its own.*

2   *The car swerved and skidded like a child riding a bike for the first time without stabilisers.*

3   *The car swerved and skidded like a duckling on a frozen pond.*

4   *The car swerved and skidded like a criminal's polygraph test.*

As with most things, reading is the cure. The fact that we, the teachers, have read lots of books will help us to see that numbers 1 and 2 are quite common comparisons in writing. It's almost as if there is a barrier of predictability that students have to break through before they can be more original. Our problem is that students don't have that natural awareness or the knowledge from experience to break through the cliché barrier; therefore, we have to help them. The simile 'like a bullet' and the onomatopoeic 'crash' are floating on the surface of their brains and are quick to fish out. What other words could you use instead of 'crash'? What could you use instead of onomatopoeia?

We need to push them to dig deeper. To think. To think of better clichés. To think of less well-known ones at least.

Breaking the connections between adjectives and nouns

We are prone to cliché. There are adjectives that we automatically associate with certain objects. If I gave you two adjectives, sturdy or delicate, to describe a table, which one would you pick? We'd all pick sturdy. We have strings of adjectives readily linked to nouns. Take the following examples:

Adjective	Noun
sturdy	table
shining	window
delicate	flower
deep	hole

The typical sentence might be:

The delicate flower stood on the sturdy table before the shining window, which was like a deep hole.

Look at what happens when you try to break the 'conditioning' of adjective and noun combinations:

The shining flower stood on the delicate table before the deep window, which was like a sturdy hole.

We make more meaningful, honest and interesting choices when we avoid the first thought, the cliché. How is that table delicate? How is a hole sturdy? And what is outside the window that makes it so dark and impenetrable? Clichéd writing is often just lazy writing. The writer picks the first word that comes to mind. This approach allows students to avoid the obvious.

Spelling out the clichés

I am grateful to Team English on Twitter for the suggestions that inspired this piece of work.[2] I asked them to tell me what clichés they often saw when asking students for a creepy piece of writing.

The dark, gloomy, scary, haunted room was cold. It had a spooky and eerie atmosphere. I could smell rotting flesh. The floorboards creaked under my footsteps. I saw blood dripping from the ceiling. I felt the hairs on the back of my neck tingle and a shiver down my spine. It got colder. My teeth were chattering so hard you could hear them.

BANG. My heart stopped. My heart literally stopped. A book had fallen on the dusty floor.

I continued to walk even though my legs had turned to jelly. I was scared.

Suddenly, my hand was grabbed by something or someone. My heart skipped a beat. I saw the zombie's face and its teeth and …

I woke up. It had all been a dream.

We're pretty clear what we want students to create, but not always as clear about what we *don't* want them to do, assuming that it's just common sense, so we don't need to mention it. Clichés are quite a difficult concept when you have little experience. Teachers can spot them a mile off because we have read so much good and bad writing. But, as our students lack this experience, they default to this method because they haven't got anything else as a point of comparison.

I like to copy this example and give it to students and tell them that each phrase is like running nails down a blackboard for me and any other reader or examiner. We then look at how they can say the same thing but make it sound better.

---

2   Find them @Team_English1 or by searching for #TeamEnglish.

Colour me

Texture and detail in writing is what gives it depth and interest. Students tend to be so obsessed with the plot they are creating that detail is forgotten. The chase is more important than the colour of the cars. A big job for English teachers is getting students to care about the detail. The fine detail. The texture. Nothing does this better than colour.

What colour T-shirt am I wearing? I am wearing a turquoise T-shirt. What kind of turquoise? Well, a light-coloured one.

The more we question it, the more detailed we get. One thing I like getting students to do is invent their own names for colours. Of course, we could easily go to the local paint store and steal some names, but I find it more satisfying if the students name their own. I like to start off by asking, 'What is the difference between these different kinds of white?'

- egg white
- paper white
- dirty white
- yellowy white
- faded white
- smudged white

If I'm honest, we rarely fully take in the colours around us. I think we have so much sensory overload daily that we focus out, so it is natural for students to not obsess about colour. However, when they do it can add something genuinely subtle to their writing.

The smudged white tablecloth had seen better days and it contrasted with the egg white of the woman's dress.

I am a fan of the novelist Patricia Highsmith and her description is quite concise. She rarely wastes an adjective. The example above has more in common with her than with the classic giants of literature. Anybody can chuck a load of adjectives at a text, but it takes a skilled writer to use an adjective in the right place to add meaning. Ideally, we need students to create effective and meaningful writing by adding one or two choice adjectives. That's why I am not too keen on giving students lengthy word lists. We want trim writing rather than bloated prose. I get students to name their own colours so that they aren't just showing off but looking to create meaning.

What colour T-shirt am I wearing? Simply, a frosted arctic blue T-shirt.

Personify me

I find that building up writing in layers is helpful. Building up a sentence one step at a time helps students explore the choices they could make. The following are a list of steps I use with students to get them to develop and extend figurative language. Instead of writing an example of personification and plonking it in a sentence, they construct a bigger, more complex piece that links across the whole sentence.

Step 1: Think of some verbs only a human would do.

Sneezes

Whispers

Stares

Grins

Smiles

Nods

Shivers

Step 2: Think of an object.

The lights

The floor

The desk

The speaker

The microphone

The projector

The chair

Step 3: Add some adjectives to the object.

The harsh, cold lights

The clean floor

The high, towering desk

The blank, tall speaker

The warm microphone

The bright projector

The silent chair

Step 4: Put some of the objects and the verbs together.

The high, towering desk stares.

The blank, tall speaker sneezes music.

The warm microphone shivers.

The silent chair smiles.

Step 5: Add a simile at the end.

The high, towering desk stares like a courtroom judge.

The blank, tall speaker sneezes music like a pneumatic drill.

The warm microphone shivers like a nervous animal.

The silent chair smiles like an assassin.

Step 6: Add just a little more detail.

The high, towering desk stares like a courtroom judge, hoping to condemn.

The blank, tall speaker sneezes music like a pneumatic drill, struggling to control itself.

The warm microphone shivers like a nervous animal, wishing it was somewhere else.

The silent chair smiles like an assassin, waiting to get ready.

Investigating similes

How much time do we honestly spend on a single aspect of writing? It is better to do one thing really well than several things badly. Yet we always seem to rush. If we want to improve aspects of writing, we need to dedicate time to it, and quality time too. I once spent two lessons working on crafting similes with a Year 9 class. We needed this time. Some might call this the mastery principle; I call it teaching. We started with several sentences featuring some pretty lame and clichéd similes.

The snow fell down like it was a blizzard.

The sword went through him like a knife through butter.

The grenade exploded like a rocket.

Linking back to the 'perfection' element of writing, we were starting at the opposite end. We started with imperfect examples. Getting students to explain why something doesn't work is easier than getting them to explain why it is effective. As a result of this, we were able to make a list of key points about what makes a good simile and formulate guidance on what they should do with their writing.

- Avoid comparing to something similar.

- Try to create some kind of emotional reaction from the simile.

- Make sure the simile isn't comical or ludicrous.

The students were self-regulating and set up their own parameters for success. They led the success criteria. The original similes then became something like the following:

The snow fell down like a widow's tears.

The sword went through him like a ghost's hand.

The grenade exploded like the birth of a star.

At this stage, students offered ideas. Again, we repeated the process and explored what would make them even better. We made another list:

- Aim for a contrast between the item described and the item compared.

- Aim for something precise and unique.

- Aim to extend the simile with more detail.

- Aim to suggest the connection between the items through detail.

Again, the students created new similes and developed them further. We repeated and repeated the process over two lessons.

The snow fell down like a widow's tears – nothing could stop the flow after years of holding back and hiding them.

The sword went through him <u>like a ghost's hand: silent and stealthily</u>.

The grenade exploded <u>like the birth of a star. Death and life held together in one split second</u>.

Sometimes, just showing students a duff example isn't enough. They have to live and breathe it to understand the issues. In one lesson, we could easily draft the same simile four or five times, but each time it gets better. Drafting isn't always about rewriting whole texts. It can be rewriting a sentence or even a phrase. The key thing is that students learn from the process, so it gets easier. They remember the experience and they develop knowledge about what unlocks a successful simile. Like an uncontrollable snowball, they pick up ideas, rules and examples. (I couldn't stop myself.)

6. MUCH ADO ABOUT MOTIFS

Teaching the structure of stories is problematic. Storytelling is a natural thing, yet when getting students to write stories we use simplistic terminology like opening, complication, crisis and resolution. When we tell stories, we inherently know what works and what doesn't. We know we have to grab the reader's interest from the start, and then we have to work at maintaining that interest to the end. Some rudimentary diagram is not going to make writing better. It hasn't for years. Never have I written the following on a student's story:

Great opening. The problem with your writing is that you haven't included a complication or a crisis. To get better, you need to add a complication and a crisis.

It is meaningless. Each story is unique and you need to give advice based on what's in front of you. What works for one will not work for another. When teaching creative writing, there's the danger that we promote the idea that stories follow a beige standard format. I read avidly and no two stories are the same. No two have an identical structure. There are simply billions of ways to tell a story. If we use sweeping brushstrokes, we get writing that is general, boring and lacking originality. Perfect writing isn't stereotypical – in fact, it is the opposite.

To help students to structure interesting stories I focus on motifs. I find it helps to use short animated films to convey the idea. YouTube and the Literacy Shed are great sources for short animated films. Literacy Shed even has the short films linked together thematically.[3] Then we explore how we can tell the story though the motif. I have successfully used the idea of a motif for dystopian fiction and got students to write about a cracked world.

Let's take a simple story, with mirrors as my motif.

What aspects of a mirror could I use?

- Reflection.

- Broken mirrors cause bad luck.

- Dirty/obscured.

- Something not right.

- Inverted.

Then I create a short plan, often visual, plotting a story around the mirror.

1   Woman gets dressed looking in a mirror.

2   Man gets dressed without looking in the mirror.

3   Oven in kitchen reflects image of the two eating, but neither is looking at or talking to the other person.

4   Man breaks the mirror when searching for something.

5   Woman decides to leave the man.

---

3   See https://www.literacyshed.com/home.html.

The mirror becomes something bigger in the structure of the story. It takes on a symbolic meaning. The fact that the man doesn't look in the mirror suggests his lack of ability to see the situation the woman is able to see. It makes for interesting storytelling. Oh, and your complication and crisis is there, hidden behind the mirror.

If you want students to write stories about 'suddenly his head was chopped off' or 'the room exploded', then insist they include a crisis in a piece of writing. I find an emotional or spiritual crisis is far more powerful and wide-reaching than a CGI-worthy explosion.

7. WRITING FROM MEMORY

My wife couldn't stand English when she was at school and said her success in exams was down to her ability to replicate one essay. She produced a really good essay for a teacher and then just repeated it again and again. There's an old saying that every-body has a book in them. What if everybody has one story or one essay? Should they be spending their years in secondary education improving it or looking to improve their ability to write hundreds?

This is contentious. Naturally, teachers want to make success easier for students and they will look for ways to unlock that success. Over the years, we have tried various approaches. The AFOREST acronym is one example. The problem was in its misuse. Students were blindsided into thinking that every paragraph must contain alliteration, fact, opinion, rhetorical questions, emotive language, statistics and tone. The writing was shaped around the devices. The content became immaterial and the use of literary techniques paramount.

Shaping writing is a problem for students. Really able students can shape and mould ideas quite deftly, but the less able struggle and will often stumble at the first step. Plus, how do you get students to revise for the writing sections of the exam? I think it's ludicrous to get them to practise exactly how to write to 'advise' and to 'review'. It's a checklist mentality that doesn't allow for much thought-shaping.

One thing I do is get them to revise something that they can shape their thinking around in the exam. Get them to revise the shape of their writing. Note, I am saying shape and not structure. Structures are rigid and immovable. Shape is foundational but malleable. Take this example for descriptive writing:

Paragraph 1

- Structure – close, closer, closest.

- List of emotions.

- Start a sentence with a simile.

- Ellipsis.

Paragraph 2

- Structure – obsess about one object in great detail, thinking about size, shape, texture and colour.

- Triplet.

- Rhetorical question.

- Colon.

Paragraph 3

- Structure – mood change.

- Personification.

- Repetition of the opening of a sentence.

- Reference to a Greek myth.

- Semicolon.

Paragraph 4

- Structure – return to the beginning.

- Contrast.

- Repetition of a word or phrase.

- Pathetic fallacy.
- Brackets.

Students learn when to put a technique, grammatical device or structural feature in a paragraph. The combination in each paragraph is important because it stops students overwriting sections and listing techniques. They learn about the combinations they could include and have an aide-memoire to prompt their writing. The content could be absolutely anything, but the writing has a balance of techniques and stylistic choices. The beauty of this is that it combats the dreaded overblown first paragraph which contains every known literary device. Take the following example:

Close to me the waves tickled the shore. Closer still was the sleeping wet dog my husband had insisted on bringing to the beach. The closest thing to me was my snoring husband. Pride, frustration, annoyance, joy and pity all competed in my heart. Like a troublesome teenager, our relationship was never predictable or controllable. Things hadn't improved by the night when ... or when he ... or even when I ...

Students can use the bullet points in any order, but they have part of a plan before they have even written a word. Then they can think about planning the structure around those bullet points. Furthermore, I add specific words and other little touches to their plans. However, I get each student to map out an individual plan each time so that the class is not replicating the same version over and over. The key thing is that they shape their writing to fit their ideas. I photocopy the plans and get students to add to and change theirs as they go along. This avoids every piece of writing being about pressing the reset button. Some students just need the confidence from a scaffold in order to write. There is nothing worse than going into an exam and not having a clue where to start on a question.

CONCLUSION

My wife has a funny approach to books. She will read the ending before the beginning. Surprisingly, she is not alone in this bizarre method. So, with this in mind, I thought I'd include a conclusion here so she can get the gist of the ideas in the book. These are my seven key underpinning principles:

1   Ideas – complex thinking should be at the heart of all English lessons. That complex thinking can be presented simply, but students should be engaged cerebrally in every lesson. Students should be reading complex texts with the hope that they recreate complex ideas in their writing.

2   Choices – students are writers and they have to become familiar with the writing process. A writer has a myriad of options at any point, and we need to work actively to help students see those choices.

3   Comparing – to understand our level of ability, we need to see where we are in relation to others. Where we want to be. Where we used to be. Think of the Roman god Janus: looking backwards and forwards at the same time. The picture of what we want to produce must be clear and placed next to where we are at the moment so we can see the steps needed to get from one to the other. Success must be evidenced so we can replicate the features of it and adapt our thinking or behaviour to allow it to occur.

4   Vocabulary – complex thinking needs complex and, more importantly, specific language.

5   Talking – we learned to talk before we learned to write, so we need to utilise this ability and allow students to see how that interfaces with writing. Talking and writing are two separate mediums, but they are closely linked. A teacher's talk can be a model for a student's writing; a student's talk can be a way for them to articulate a complex idea in preparation for writing.

6   Structure – we all crave structure and systematic approaches to solving problems. The same applies in English. A system for spelling, vocabulary,

sentence structure and other aspects will help the students cope with problems and save the teacher time, effort and energy.

7   Experiences – every child in a classroom has had different life experiences. Teaching should be about providing experiences that are familiar to all: shared experiences which help us to make sense of the world.

The joy of teaching is that it is never finished. We are always learning. The problem with teaching is that you can never really tick off a job. A simple job can spiral and dominate even your 'free' time. That's why it is so hard to conclude this book, because we all aspire for a version of perfection. A long time ago, I twigged that perfection isn't really the goal in teaching. Aiming for perfection is the goal in itself. There has never been, nor will there be, a year in which 100% of students achieve full marks. We are just trying to be better than last year. Each year, I aim to be better than the last. A good teacher, in my opinion, is one who is always learning from their mistakes and wanting to get better. That isn't something you can quantify or measure in this world of accountability.

If you have changed or improved one thing in the classroom as a result of this book, then I am a happy man.

AFTERWORD

Being a teacher of English is one of the best jobs there is; it's profoundly important whether you are in a secondary school department or it's one of your many hats as a primary practitioner. One of the beauties of it is that, unlike other subjects, we don't teach the same thing each year. Each time we read a novel, poem or play it becomes something new and different. Our subject changes because the context we are teaching in changes. The political situation in America changes the way students see power in texts. The contemporary social disparity between poor and rich makes us see Victorian novels as freshly relevant. Each teacher or student brings something new to the study of literature. No two English lessons are ever the same. No two English teachers are the same. No two students' experiences of English are the same. Literature is too closely linked to the reader and their experiences.

Teachers are some of the best people in the world. They have wit, humour and insight; plus, they have the best put-downs ever. They are the thinkers. They are the dreamers. They are the empathisers who understand people and the world around them. They are quintessentially human.

In *The Merchant of Venice*, Shylock says the following in response to the injustice he has suffered:

> *I am a Jew. Hath not a Jew eyes? Hath not a Jew hands, organs, dimensions, senses, affections, passions? Fed with the same food, hurt with the same weapons, subject to the same diseases, healed by the same means, warmed and cooled by the same winter and summer, as a Christian is? If you prick us, do we not bleed? If you tickle us, do we not laugh? If you poison us, do we not die? And if you wrong us, shall we not revenge? If we are like you in the rest, we will resemble you in that. If a Jew wrong a Christian, what is his humility? Revenge. If a Christian wrong a Jew, what should his sufferance be by Christian example? Why, revenge. The villany you teach me, I will execute, and it shall go hard but I will better the instruction.*[1]

---

1   W. Shakespeare, *The Merchant of Venice* (Project Gutenberg ebook edition, 2000 [1596]). Available at: http://www.gutenberg.org/cache/epub/2243/pg2243-images.html.

Shylock, like us, lived in a divided world. He saw connections where others didn't. Shakespeare showed us that we have far more in common than we do differences, and how we are shaped by the people around us. I think this is a great point to end with. Shylock became embittered because of the experiences he lived through. It is vital that English teachers do not give in to such a temptation.

The teenage years are monumental in shaping a person. Our ideas and thoughts, I feel, take root here and linger. I am about to enter my fourth decade, but I can remember *Hamlet* vividly from my teenage lessons. We have a duty, alongside our students' parents, to shape and change them for life: emotionally, intellectually and morally. We help students to think and feel. We help them to reflect on their actions. We hold a mirror to society and help them to see how they can make it better. We help them to think and feel before they act. What other subject does that?

Never underestimate your role, your duty and your power in the English classroom.

REFERENCES AND FURTHER READING

AQA. *GCSE English Language Paper 2 Writer's Viewpoints and Perspectives: Report on the Examination*, 8700, June 2017. Available at: https://filestore.aqa.org.uk/sample-papers-and-mark-schemes/2017/june/AQA-87002-WRE-JUN17.PDF.

AQA. *GCSE English Literature (8702) Specification*, Version 1.1, 23 September 2014. Available at: https://filestore.aqa.org.uk/resources/english/specifications/AQA-8702-SP-2015.PDF.

AQA. *GCSE English Literature (8702): Poems Past and Present: poetry anthology*, Version 1.0, June 2015 (Cambridge: Cambridge University Press, 2015).

Blake, W. 'London', in *Songs of Innocence and Songs of Experience* (Project Gutenberg ebook edition, 2008 [London: R. Brimley Johnson, 1901]), p. 58. Available at: http://www.gutenberg.org/files/1934/1934-h/1934-h.htm#page58.

Blake, W. 'The Tiger', in *Songs of Innocence and Songs of Experience* (Project Gutenberg ebook edition, 2008 [London: R. Brimley Johnson, 1901]), pp. 51–52. Available at: http://www.gutenberg.org/files/1934/1934-h/1934-h.htm#page51.

Browning, R. 'Porphyria's Lover', in H. E. Scudder (ed.), *The Complete Poetic and Dramatic Works of Robert Browning* (Project Gutenberg ebook edition, 2016 [Cambridge, MA: The Riverside Press, 1895]), p. 286. Available at: http://www.gutenberg.org/files/50954/50954-h/50954-h.htm.

Brownjohn, S. *Does It Have to Rhyme? Teaching Children to Write Poetry* (London: Hodder Education, 1980).

Brownjohn, S. *The Poet's Craft: A Handbook of Rhyme, Metre and Verse* (London: Hodder Education, 2002).

Brownjohn, S. *To Rhyme or Not to Rhyme: Teaching Children to Write Poetry* (London: Hodder Education, 1994).

Bryson, B. *Shakespeare* (London: Harper, 2016).

Clark, R. P. *Writing Tools: 50 Essential Strategies for Every Writer* (London: Little, Brown and Company, 2008).

Conan Doyle, A. *The Sign of the Four* (Project Gutenberg ebook edition, 2008 [1890]). Available at: http://www.gutenberg.org/files/2097/2097-h/2097-h.htm.

Crystal, B. *Shakespeare on Toast: Getting a Taste for the Bard* (London: Icon Books, 2009).

Crystal, B. *Springboard Shakespeare: Macbeth* (London: Bloomsbury, 2013).

Curtis, C. Revision cards, *Learning from My Mistakes* [blog] (4 January 2018). Available at: http://learningfrommymistakesenglish.blogspot.co.uk/2018/01/revision-cards.html.

Dickens, C. *A Christmas Carol* (Project Gutenberg ebook edition, 2006 [New York: The Platt & Peck Co., 1905]). Available at: http://www.gutenberg.org/files/19337/19337-h/19337-h.htm.

Dickens, C. *A Tale of Two Cities* (Project Gutenberg ebook edition, 2004 [1859]). Available at: http://www.gutenberg.org/files/98/98-h/98-h.htm.

Dickens, C. *Great Expectations* (Project Gutenberg ebook edition, 2008 [1867]). Available at: http://www.gutenberg.org/files/1400/1400-h/1400-h.htm.

Dickens, C. *Oliver Twist* (Project Gutenberg ebook edition, 1996 [1837]). Available at: http://www.gutenberg.org/files/730/730-h/730-h.htm.

Duffy, C. A. 'War Photographer', in *Standing Female Nude* (London: Anvil Press Poetry, 1985), p. 49.

Fish, S. *How to Write a Sentence: And How to Read One* (New York: HarperCollins, 2012).

Forsyth, M. *The Elements of Eloquence: How to Turn the Perfect English Phrase* (London: Icon Books Ltd, 2016).

Fry, S. *The Ode Less Travelled: Unlocking the Poet Within* (London: Arrow, 2007).

Gibson, R. *Teaching Shakespeare* (Cambridge: Cambridge University Press, 1998).

Greer, G. *Shakespeare: A Very Short Introduction* (Oxford: Oxford University Press, 2002).

Guardian, The. The shot that nearly killed me: war photographers – a special report (18 June 2011). Available at: https://www.theguardian.com/media/2011/jun/18/war-photographers-special-report.

Guardian, The. The Titanic is sunk, with great loss of life (16 April 1912). Available at: https://www.theguardian.com/news/1912/apr/16/leadersandreply.mainsection.

Jenkinson, M. and Gullifer, R. *How Poems Work: Meanings, Techniques and Effects in 100 Poems from* Beowulf *to the Iraq War* by (Woodbridge: John Catt Educational, 2018).

Jonson, B. 'On My First Son', in *Discoveries Made Upon Men and Matter and Some Poems* (Project Gutenberg ebook edition, 2014 [London: Cassell & Company, 1892]). Available at: http://www.gutenberg.org/files/5134/5134-h/5134-h.htm.

Kermode, F. *Shakespeare's Language* (London: Penguin, 2001).

Kipling, R. 'Tommy', in *The Works of Rudyard Kipling: One Volume Edition* (Project Gutenberg ebook edition, 2000 [1914]). Available at: http://www.gutenberg.org/files/2334/2334-h/2334-h.htm#link2H_4_0058.

Leith, S. *You Talkin' to Me: Rhetoric from Aristotle to Obama* (London: Profile Books, 2012).

Lemov, D., Driggs, C. and Woolway, E. *Reading Reconsidered: A Practical Guide to Rigorous Literacy Instruction* (San Francisco, CA: Jossey-Bass, 2016).

London, J. *The People of the Abyss* (Project Gutenberg ebook edition, 2005 [Edinburgh: Thomas Nelson and Sons, 1903]). Available at: http://www.gutenberg.org/files/1688/1688-h/1688-h.htm.

McCormick, I. *The Art of Connection: The Social Life of Sentences* (CreateSpace, 2013).

Murphy, J. and Murphy, D. *Think Reading: What Every Secondary Teacher Needs to Know About Reading* (Woodbridge: John Catt Educational, 2018).

Owen, W. 'Dulce et Decorum est' (Project Gutenberg ebook edition, 2008 [1920]). Available at: http://www.gutenberg.org/files/1034/1034-h/1034-h.htm.

Owen, W. 'Futility', in *Poems* (Project Gutenberg ebook edition, 2008 [1918]). Available at: http://www.gutenberg.org/files/1034/1034-h/1034-h.htm#link2H_4_0022.

Peat, A. *Writing Exciting Sentences: Age Seven Plus* (Biddulph: Creative Educational Press, 2008).

Pieper, K. *Reading for Pleasure: A Passport to Everywhere* (Carmarthen: Independent Thinking Press, 2016).

Priestley, J. B. *An Inspector Calls* (London: Heinemann, 1992 [1945]).

Prose, F. *Reading Like a Writer: A Guide for People Who Love Books and for Those Who Want to Write Them* (London: Union Books, 2006).

Quigley, A. *Closing the Vocabulary Gap* (Abingdon: Routledge, 2018).

Quigley, A. *Teach Now! English: Becoming a Great English Teacher* (Abingdon: Routledge, 2014).

Roberts, M. A quick word retrieval practice for single word quotations, *Mark Roberts Teach* [blog] (25 November 2017). Available at: https://markrobertsteach.wordpress.com/2017/11/25/a-quick-word-retrieval-practice-for-single-word-quotations/.

Robinson, M. *Trivium 21c: Preparing Young People for the Future with Lessons from the Past* (Carmarthen: Independent Thinking Press, 2016).

Robinson, M. *Trivium in Practice* (Carmarthen: Independent Thinking Press, 2013).

Rossetti, C. 'Song', in *Goblin Market, The Prince's Progress, and Other Poems* (Project Gutenberg ebook edition, 2008 [London: Macmillan and Co., 1862]). Available at: http://www.gutenberg.org/cache/epub/16950/pg16950-images.html.

Shakespeare, W. *Julius Caesar* (Ware: Wordsworth Classics, 1992 [1599]).

Shakespeare, W. *Macbeth* (Project Gutenberg ebook edition, 1998 [1606]). Available at: http://www.gutenberg.org/cache/epub/1533/pg1533-images.html.

Shakespeare, W. *Romeo and Juliet* (Ware: Wordsworth Classics, 1992 [1595]).

Shakespeare, W. *The Merchant of Venice* (Project Gutenberg ebook edition, 2000 [1596]). Available at: http://www.gutenberg.org/cache/epub/2243/pg2243-images.html.

Shelley, P. B. 'Ozymandias', in T. Hutchinson (ed.), *The Complete Poetical Works of Percy Bysshe Shelley Volume II* (Project Gutenberg ebook edition, 2003 [Oxford: Oxford University Press, 1914, poem first published 1818]). Available at: http://www.gutenberg.org/cache/epub/4798/pg4798-images.html.

Spalding, C. Teaching ideas: what has worked for me recently?, *Teacher's Notes* [blog] (1 May 2017). Available at: http://mrscspalding.blogspot.com/2017/05/teaching-ideas-what-has-worked-for-me.html.

Steinbeck, J. *Of Mice and Men* (New York: Penguin, 1993 [1937]).

Stevenson, R. L. The old pacific capital, in *Across the Plains with Other Memories and Essays* (Project Gutenberg ebook edition, 2013 [London: Chatto & Windus, 1915]), pp. 51–71. Available at: https://www.gutenberg.org/files/614/614-h/614-h.htm#page51.

Tennyson, Lord A. 'The Charge of the Light Brigade', in *Maud, and Other Poems, by Alfred Tennyson* (Project Gutenberg ebook edition, 2018 [London: Edward Moxon & Co., 1859]). Available at: http://www.gutenberg.org/cache/epub/56913/pg56913-images.html.

Tennyson, Lord A. 'The Eagle', in J. C. Collins (ed.), *The Early Poems of Alfred Lord Tennyson* (Project Gutenberg ebook edition, 2012 [1851]). Available at: http://www.gutenberg.org/files/8601/8601-h/8601-h.htm#section96.

Tennyson, Lord A. 'The Kraken', in J. C. Collins (ed.), *The Early Poems of Alfred Lord Tennyson* (Project Gutenberg ebook edition, 2012 [1851]). Available at: http://www.gutenberg.org/files/8601/8601-h/8601-h.htm#section125.

Tharby, A. English teaching and the problem with knowledge, *Reflecting English* [blog] (26 October 2014). Available at: https://reflectingenglish.wordpress.com/2014/10/26/english-teaching-and-the-problem-with-knowledge/.

Tharby, A. *Making Every English Lesson Count: Six Principles to Support Great Reading and Writing* (Carmarthen: Crown House Publishing, 2017).

Theune, M. (ed.). *Structure and Surprise: Engaging Poetic Turns* (New York: Teachers and Writers Collaborative, 2007).

Van Doren, M. *Macbeth*. In L. F. Dean (ed.), *Shakespeare: Modern Essays in Criticism* (Oxford: Oxford University Press, 1967), pp. 346–360.

Whitman, W. 'After the Sea-Ship', in *Leaves of Grass* (Project Gutenberg ebook edition, 2008 [1855]). Available at: http://www.gutenberg.org/files/1322/1322-h/1322-h.htm#link2H_4_0113.

RECOMMENDED WEBSITES

I am a big believer in exploring what others do in the classroom. I am indebted to Twitter, particularly Team English, for their ideas, support and enthusiasm over the years. Other sources of good ideas are:

Alex Quigley: https://www.theconfidentteacher.com/

Andy Tharby: https://reflectingenglish.wordpress.com/

Becky Wood: https://justateacherstandinginfrontofaclass.wordpress.com/

Caroline Spalding: http://mrscspalding.blogspot.co.uk/

David Bunker: https://mrbunkeredu.wordpress.com/

David Didau: http://www.learningspy.co.uk/

Doug Wise: http://www.douglaswise.co.uk/

Fiona Ritson: www.alwayslearningweb.wordpress.com/

Freya Odell: https://wheninromeeng.wordpress.com/general-resources/

Geoff Barton: www.geoffbarton.co.uk/teacher-resources.php

James Theo: https://othmarstrombone.wordpress.com/

Jenn Ludgate: https://littlemisslud.wordpress.com/

Jo Facer: https://readingallthebooks.com/

Jonathan Peel: http://www.jwpblog.wordpress.com/

Lance Hanson: https://mrhansonsenglish.wordpress.com/

Louisa Enstone: https://www.literaturedaydreams.com/

Mark Miller: www.thegoldfishbowl.edublogs.org/

Mark Roberts: https://markrobertsteach.wordpress.com/

Matt Pinkett: www.allearssite.wordpress.com

Nick Wells: https://englishremnantworld.wordpress.com/

Nikki Carlin: https://noopuddles.wordpress.com/

Phil Stock: https://joeybagstock.wordpress.com/

Rebecca Foster: https://thelearningprofession.wordpress.com/

Sarah Barker: https://thestableoyster.wordpress.com/
Susan Strachan: https://susansenglish.wordpress.com/

The list is always evolving, and I am always adding to it. The wealth of ideas, resources and approaches out there is endless.

INDEX

200 word challenge 71–73

A Christmas Carol 54, 79, 84–85, 93, 95, 97, 112, 153, 165, 170–171
A Tale of Two Cities 54
adjectives 98–99, 119, 120, 135–136, 189–190, 195, 199, 222–223, 225, 226
adverbs 67, 97, 118, 119, 120, 165–167, 188, 189, 190, 199
AFOREST 53, 65, 66, 231
'After the Sea-Ship' 24–25
An Inspector Calls 40, 113–115, 116, 161, 167–168
Animal Farm 75
AQA 10, 14, 131
Austen, Jane 65, 208

Banks, Ian 53
Blake, W. 12–14, 17, 18–19, 25, 26, 49
Blyton, Enid 52
Bradbury, Ray 53
Brontë, Charlotte 75
Browning, R. 33–36, 48

Carter, Angela 53
Christie, Agatha 52
clauses 62, 188, 191–192, 198, 201
  conditional clause 191, 192
  main clause 191, 192
  parenthetical clause 198
  relative clause 201
  subordinate clause 191
cliché 100, 211, 212, 220–227
  clichéd writing 220–229
Coleridge, Samuel Taylor 27, 48
Conan Doyle, A. 193–194, 195, 196–198
Conrad, Joseph 53

Crystal, B. 152
Crystal, David 188

Dahl, Roald 22, 53
Diary of a Wimpy Kid 86
Dickens, C. 18, 22, 52, 53, 54, 75, 85, 87, 92, 95, 97, 100, 112, 153, 154, 164, 165, 166, 167, 176, 177, 217
Doctor Who 125
drafts 52, 110–111, 181–182, 206, 229
  of writers' works 22
  redrafting 52, 207
Duffy, C.A. 10, 48, 49
'Dulce et Decorum est' 8–9

'Futility' 20, 21–22

Golding, William 63, 75, 86–87, 167
grammar 62–63, 97–98, 105, 187–202
Great Expectations 75, 79, 164–165, 217
Guardian, The 11, 132

Hamlet 141, 143, 238
handwriting 184, 185–186
Hemingway, Ernest 53
Highsmith, Patricia 53, 225
homework 58, 104, 106, 107, 183

'In Memoriam' 27
interpretation 16, 23, 46, 113, 114, 115, 118, 120, 130, 164–165, 167–169, 170
  interpretation lists 169

Jane Eyre 75, 76, 106
Jonson, Ben 9
Julius Caesar 150–152, 153–154

King, Stephen 53
Kipling, R. 27, 48
knowledge organiser 44–47, 78, 80–83

lists 43, 44, 65–69, 84, 93, 95–96, 105, 106, 119, 136, 146, 156–157, 173–174, 183, 190, 214, 225, 228
list of poems 48–49
'London' 14, 18–19, 23, 24, 25, 26
London, J. 129
Lord of the Flies 63, 75, 86, 102–104, 167

Macbeth 42, 68, 106, 107, 115–116, 121–122, 123, 141, 142–143, 145, 173–174
metaphors 25–26, 46, 113–116, 148, 152
modelling 32, 40, 52, 57–58, 90, 97, 116–117, 186, 194, 212, 213, 235
  model and read aloud 69–70
  modelling thinking 174–177
  modelling sentences 196–198
motifs 229–231
Much Ado About Nothing 68, 141, 175
multiple-choice analysis 164–165

noun phrases 195–196, 201
nouns 135–136, 172, 189–191, 195–196, 222
  abstract 15, 95–96, 98, 131–132
  proper 193, 202

Of Mice and Men 77–78, 80–83
Oliver Twist 18, 75, 92, 154
'On My First Son' 9

opinion 111, 133, 134, 139, 164, 172, 173–174
Orwell, George 11, 53, 75
Owen, W. 8, 20, 21, 106, 119
'Ozymandias' 14, 45, 200–201

Paivio, Allan 88
paragraphs 54, 59–61, 91, 112–113, 116–117, 154, 175–176, 194, 205–206, 207, 218, 232–233
parents 4, 8, 76, 163, 180, 188, 238
Peat, A. 57–58, 59, 60
PEE model 112, 123, 177
personification 87, 115, 225–227, 232
poetry 7–49, 138, 202
  'blackout poetry' 86
  central question 12–15
  choices 17–25
  connection 7–11, 14, 23, 32, 38, 40
  emotions 8, 9–11, 40
  inference words 15–17, 131–132
  knowledge of poems and styles 44–49
  layering 37–38
  manifesto 7–8
  perspective 11, 22–23, 28, 86
  poetic structure 84–86
  rhyme 25–26, 41
  sonnets and voltas 39–40
  syllables 40–44
  verse and free verse 23–25
'Porphyria's Lover' 33–37
Priestley, J. B. 114, 166
pronouns 149–152, 171–172, 193
punctuation 58, 62–65, 181, 182, 191–192, 205, 206
Punctuation Pyramid 62, 64

quotations 44, 45, 72, 99, 115, 123, 164, 165, 169–171, 176
  single-word quotations 120, 154
Quigley, A. 107

repetition 47, 87, 148, 152, 213, 218–219, 232
resources 2–3, 4, 59, 243–244
Rowling, J. K. 22, 53
Roberts, M. 170
Romeo and Juliet 106, 144, 145–146, 149, 154, 155–162
Rossetti, C. 40–41

Saki 53
sentences 54, 57–59, 96, 101, 104, 118, 176, 188, 190–199, 201, 207, 210–213, 216
  complex sentences 62, 191–192, 198
  conditional sentences 62
  multi-clause sentences 54
  sentence stems 122, 127, 175, 212
  sentence structure 47, 59, 196, 236
  simple sentences 54
Shakespeare, W. 8, 42, 76, 86, 123, 141–162, 237–238
Shelley, P. B. 14, 201
similes 25–26, 46, 87, 115, 163, 188, 220–221, 227–229, 232
'Song' 40–42, 43–44
SPaG (spelling, punctuation and grammar) 62
Spalding, C. 118
spelling 179–180, 180–181, 183, 235–236
  spelling test 107, 179
Star Trek 125
Steinbeck, J. 53, 77, 78, 81, 92, 166

Stevenson, Robert Louis 22, 75, 135, 166
subject/object 193–194
summarising 16, 32, 44, 96, 131–133, 145, 146

technology 3
Tennyson, Lord A. 14, 16, 27, 30–31
Tharby, A. 168
'The Charge of the Light Brigade' 14
'The Eagle' 16–17
'The Kraken' 30–31
The Merchant of Venice 2, 237–238
The old pacific capital 135
'The Rime of the Ancient Mariner' 26, 27
The Sign of the Four 193–194, 195, 196–197
'The Tiger' 12–14, 15, 16, 17
Theune, M. 39
To Kill a Mockingbird 77
'Tommy' 27, 28–30
Treasure Island 22, 75, 166

Van Doren, Mark 123
verb phrases 195–196
verbs 19, 98, 114, 119, 122, 135–136, 189–190, 193, 214, 220, 225, 226

vocabulary 15–17, 20, 45, 83, 89, 91, 102–107, 114, 133, 153, 235

'War Photographer' 10–11
Whitman, W. 24–25
Wilson, Jacqueline 86
Wilson, Ros 62
word classification 97, 98–99, 189–191